LEX CREDENDI

LEX CREDENDI

A SEQUEL TO
LEX ORANDI

BY

GEORGE TYRRELL

AUTHOR OF "NOVA ET VETERA," "HARD SAYINGS,"
ETC.

"LOOKING UNTO JESUS, THE AUTHOR AND FINISHER
OF OUR FAITH."—*Heb.* XI.

NEW IMPRESSION

WIPF & STOCK · Eugene, Oregon

Wipf and Stock Publishers
199 W 8th Ave, Suite 3
Eugene, OR 97401

Lex Credendi
A Sequel to Lex Orandi
By Tyrrell, George, SJ
ISBN 13: 978-1-60608-390-1
Publication date 02/04/2009
Previously published by Longmans, Green and Co., 1907

CONTENTS

PART I

"THE SPIRIT OF CHRIST"

		PAGE
I.	THE SCOPE	1
II.	THE METHOD	4
III.	THE MEANING OF "SPIRIT"	8
IV.	CHRIST'S SPIRIT AS FEELING	15
V.	CHRIST "ACCORDING TO THE SPIRIT"	21
VI.	SENTIMENTALISM	25
VII.	"MYSTICALITY"	31
VIII.	"PRACTICALITY"	38
IX.	"CARITAS DEI"	43
X.	"NEW TESTAMENT CHRISTIANITY"	47
XI.	HOLINESS AND TRUTH	54
XII.	THE PERFECTION OF MANHOOD	61
XIII.	THE SUPERMAN, FALSE AND TRUE	68
XIV.	RÉSUMÉ	72

PART II

THE PRAYER OF CHRIST

I.	THE PERFECT PRAYER	82
II.	DEFECTIVE TYPES	88
III.	THE INVOCATION	101

IV.	THE FIRST PETITION		132
V.	THE SECOND PETITION		151
VI.	THE THIRD PETITION		178
VII.	THE FOURTH PETITION		199
VIII.	THE FIFTH PETITION		214
IX.	THE SIXTH PETITION		227
X.	THE SEVENTH PETITION		235
XI.	RESULTS		241

CONCLUSION—LEX ORANDI 251

PREFACE

THE title which I have chosen for this volume needs some explanation. In "Lex Orandi" I endeavoured to show how the Christian Creed had been, not entirely, but principally shaped by the exigencies of the devout life; and how it ought therefore to be viewed primarily as a Law of Prayer or of practical devotion, and only secondarily as a theology. My intention was far more practical than apologetic. I wrote in the interest of that growing number of earnestly religious persons whose impatience with theological disputes, and whose conviction that the Gospel means deeds rather than words or theories, lead them to look upon the Creed with a cold eye; to view it as belonging more to the outward life of the Visible Church than to the inward life of the individual Christian; to regard it as the sword of militant orthodoxy rather than as a subtle factor of the very same Spirit of Charity in whose name they would fain thrust that dividing sword into its scabbard. There (and still more explicitly elsewhere in subsequent occasional articles and reviews) I emphasized the importance of distinguishing between the "substance" of the Creed, which we owe to revelation, and whose proper vehicle of expression is the language of prophecy and mystery rather than that of science or philosophy, and that "form" which the same Creed has necessarily and rightly received in consequence of becoming an object of theological reflection. Revelation offers us mysteries of Faith; theology endeavours to translate them from the language of prophecy into that of science, and to harmonize these translations with the whole system of our understanding. It is the "substance" of the Creed and not its "form" that Faith lays hold of as the food of the soul, the Bread of Life, the Word of God. If we accept the form it is only because we cannot draw water without a vessel. In the *Te Deum* and in other hymns and canticles of the Church we possess the Christian Creed more nearly in the prophetic language of revelation, and divested to a great extent of its theological setting. There we find it exercising its principal and original function of appealing, not so much to the understanding as to the imagination; not so much to the explicit reason of the mind as to the implicit reason of the heart. Thus we not only may and ought to, but we actually do separate the substance of the Creed from its theological or scientific form.

Again, in the interests of devotion, I frequently insisted on the danger of treating disjointed fragments or articulations of the Creed as independent wholes, intelligible and spiritually valuable even when divorced from their context. The possibility of doing so is the result of giving (as we are prone to do) objective value to the distinctions and divisions of scientific reflection—of transferring to the living reality the form that belongs merely to our understanding of it. Yet what Faith embraces is never the severed part, but that same whole which is also the indivisible object of Hope and Love. The mind, indeed, may abstract, and analyse, and dissect; it may give a fictitious completeness to what are really fragments; but it is only the unbroken unity of the living whole which appeals to the heart—and Faith is of the heart. To this or that separate article we may give a theological assent with our mind; but the assent of Faith belongs to it only as vitally one with the complete object of Faith, which is the mystery of the Kingdom of God. In this mystery all others are included; from this they get their meaning and unity; apart, they may live for theological thought, but they are dead for Faith.

In substance, our Creed is but the expression of that conception of God and His Kingdom which is the light of our spiritual life—a conception constitutive of that same indivisible life which is at once Vision, Feeling, and Will according as it is viewed from different angles. By one and the same act we identify ourselves with God, who, viewed as Truth, Might, or Goodness, characterizes that act as one of Faith, Hope, or Charity respectively. Faith is the right orientation of the spirit in relation to its end and action, and the Creed is primarily the verbal expression of this adjustment—the correspondence is that of words to things; of abstract signs to the inexhaustible fulness and complexity of a concrete spiritual act.

But if its purpose is the perfection and spiritual education of the individual believer, it attains this end only because it is the expression of the collective spiritual life of the Church at large—which life is normal and authoritative for the individual, and must be appropriated by him before any sort of healthy personality of belief can be developed. In no two souls could the words of the Creed stand for quite the same thing, while to the Reader of Hearts our divergencies of conception, veiled from us by the coarse medium of language, widen out indefinitely and make inward heretics of us all. Even were perfect uniformity of inward belief conceivable, no language, however flexible and subtle, no test, however cunningly devised, could possibly prove its existence.

It is not then directly as an expression of my own private judgment and spiritual orientation that I say the *Credo*, but as an expression of the Church's collective Faith, which I desire to share and appropriate, and which I acknowledge as a rule or norm. I say it as a quasi-sacramental act of association with the corporate life of the Christian people, past, present, and future. It is the "I" of the whole Church which finds voice in in me and each of her members. "Credimus," Πιστεύομεν, "We believe," was the older formula, as it is that of the *Te Deum*, and it gives us the true sense of the newer.

But since this is so, it is plain that in reciting the Creed I do not address myself to, or profess to be in inward agreement with, any other individual or school or passing phase of theological thought; that none of these have any more right to rule my spirit than I have to rule theirs; that the only norm I acknowledge is that to which they must defer as well as I—that of the slowly forming, but divinely guided, mind of the living Church of all times and places, of which mind the Creed in its present form is the only authorized expression. To say that such a norm is necessarily indefinite and ambiguous in many respects, is only to say that it is living and progressive.

By these and similar considerations I strove to show that those whose impatience of theology drove them to a somewhat onesidedly practical and utilitarian conception of religion, could not afford to dispense with creeds and dogmas, since these were really the presuppositions (however subtle and implicit) of all life and action, and had been largely shaped in the interests of feeling and practice. In other words, I tried to show that the Creed was primarily a *Lex Orandi*—a law of prayer and of the spiritual life. In this volume I pursue much the same theme, strengthening some of the positions taken up in "Lex Orandi," criticizing and establishing some of its underlying assumptions, defending myself against certain misunderstandings due to the fact that in addressing myself largely to "Pragmatists" I seemed to some—in spite of fairly explicit precautions—to accept their doctrines far more than I do.

But as I called the former book "Lex Orandi" because it dealt with the Creed under its aspect of a rule of prayer, so I may call this book "Lex Credendi," for in substance it is a treatment of the Lord's Prayer viewed as the rule and criterion of pure doctrine—as the living expression of that Christian spirit whereof Faith in God and His Kingdom, together with Hope and Charity, is a constituent factor. As no single article of Faith is rightly intelligible torn apart from the living organism of truth which it helps to constitute, so neither is Faith itself fully intelligible as considered apart from Hope and Charity, its correlatives, which together with it constitute one simple and really indivisible life of the spirit. Our grasp on Faith is simply included in our grasp on that life in its totality—in our grasp on God, who is the object at once of our Faith, Hope, and Love. Because it is bound up, in our past experience, with our supernatural life, we hold to the Christian Creed in its entirety by the same act wherewith we hold to God. For it is the form or shape in which the Divine is presented to us and apprehended by us.

Far surer, therefore, and truer than any mental or oral expression which we can give to our belief as separated by abstraction from the concrete unity of our spiritual life, is the expression which it receives in every exercise of that life in its fulness. "By their fruits ye shall know them"; it is not by what a man says he believes (or disbelieves), or by what he explicitly and consciously thinks he believes, but by the Faith implicit in his spontaneous life and action and in the whole orientation of his feeling and will that the deep, subconscious convictions of his heart find true utterance. If "the heart has its reasons," it has also its language, often at strife with that of the lips—eloquent when these are silent, dumb when they are busiest. No explicit utterance of the Christian Faith can ever hope to equal the implicit utterance it finds in that Prayer which burst forth from the depth of Christ's heart and which is the embodiment of the spiritual life in its concrete fulness. There in truth we have the supreme rule and criterion of Faith, the divinely sanctioned *Lex Credendi* —no ready solvent indeed for theological controversies, but a law that lifts the heart to a higher plane where it can abide in peace, unaffected by the alternations of intellectual light and obscurity.

Surely it is well to insist on these truisms at a time when sun and moon are darkened, and when our guiding stars are falling from heaven, and the once solid earth trembles beneath our feet, and the indolent hearts of men of little faith are failing them for fear of the tribulation that threatens their spiritual peace and tranquillity. It is well at such a time to see that we do not confound things so different as theological confusion and shipwreck of

Faith ; or hold ourselves bankrupt because we have mislaid the mere symbol of a wealth that is still safely treasured in the secret chamber of our heart, and vouched for by every instinctive exercise of the Christian life.

Faith in God the Rewarder, or rather the Reward, of them that seek Him is, according to even the most rigid theology, the saving substance of the Creed wherein all its further determinations are enfolded, as are the form, fragrance, and glory of the full-blown flower in the first rudiments of its green bud. If we hold this we hold all ; for there is no real "unfaith" *of the heart* as to any particular revealed truth or truths which would not be instantly fatal to that deepest truth in which they are all rooted and involved, and which finds implicit utterance in the Lord's Prayer, in the *Lex Credendi*.

But do we really hold it?

This, as has been said, is no question as to our theology or religious philosophy, but as to our whole practical attitude towards life; as to our spiritual character and orientation. Faith in God means faith in Conscience, in Sincerity, in Truth—blind faith in what neither reasoning nor experience can justify, but what is whispered and revealed to the heart, namely, that Truth and Right must at last prevail; that apart from all other rewards and irrespective of all consequences, these are the only ends claiming our absolute and unconditional self-subjection, and compared with which all others are vain and illusory. However variously determined and diversely applied, these are the ultimate ends for which the saints, prophets, and martyrs of all times and places have lived, suffered, and died, and which unite them into one invisible society, one world-wide mystical Christ, one ceaseless sacrifice for the world's salvation. Faith in God means faith in Christ crucified, in His method, His spirit, His way; in His fearless attitude towards the worldly, in His uncompromising truthfulness and sincerity which triumphed most in the moment of His extremest disaster.

With this Faith we need not fear the temporary obscuration or confusion of some of our theological conceptions at a time when the publicly notorious disputes between critical and theological experts as to the historical or philosophical values of revealed truths and mysteries (i.e. as to the precise translation of the language of prophecy into that of science) make it quite impossible for us, who are in no sense experts, to arrive at a decision. At such a time we may firmly decline to stand an examination in history or theology or physics; the Church is not an university or a school. We may content ourselves with Faith in the unbroken totality of revelation as presented to us in its original and essential form of "prophetic truth"; and we may refuse to express any opinion on the various attempts which have been made, especially of late, to translate that prophecy into the language of exact thought.

Enough that we hold the root of the matter, from

which, when the sharp winter of healthy criticism has fulfilled its divine mission, a gentler spring will call forth stalk, leaf, and flower in due season: "quia post hiemem sequitur aestas; post mortem redit dies; et post tempestatem, magna serenitas" ("Imitatio Christi," lib. II, ch. 8).

G. TYRRELL

FREIBURG i. BR.
    7 *March*, 1906

NOTE

SEVERAL of the chapters of this book have appeared in "The Dolphin" (now no more) under the title, "The Spirit of Christ"; and later in "The Catholic World" under the title, "The Prayer of Christ." Except the Preface, the whole was finished some months ago; hence none of the elucidations of "Lex Orandi" have been made in deference to criticisms that have since appeared. They are in no sense corrections, but only elucidations of points there lightly touched, though not fully developed, or, at most, completions of what had no pretence of being more than a rough essay. Such are, e.g. (1) the renewed insistence on the fundamental difference between the "Pragmatism" of Christ and the philosophy which to-day goes by that name, and with which it has else so much in common; (2) the iterated recognition of the rights of a sane and free theology ministering to, but no wise to be confounded with, revelation, whose prophetic truth it endeavours to translate into exact language and to reconcile with the ever-varying requirements of contemporary knowledge; (3) the emphasis of the fact that some kind of, at least implicit, dogmatic (but not necessarily theological) conception is the presupposition of even the simplest and most elementary religious experience; (4) the exposition of the essential difference between the Catholic and the non-Catholic forms of Christianity which lies in the frank appropriation by the former of the fruits of the general religious process of humanity, gathered together in the religious syncretism of the Roman Empire, of which fruits Judaism contributed but a part—albeit a principal part. In other words, the insistence on the supra-sectarian character which at least in principle distinguishes from all particular religions that Catholicism which allows some degree of supernatural inspiration to every genuine religious utterance of mankind according to its strength and quality; which sees in the totality of such utterances the ever-inadequate expression of That which seeks to reveal Itself to the human spirit as far as the limited receptivity of that spirit will permit; a Sun whose light struggles to us through clouds of varying density, from the most darkly impenetrable to the most brilliantly luminous, but whose face and form we have never beheld; (5) the definitive abandonment of the two notions of ecclesiastical and theological development, whose insufficiency I discussed in an article, "Semper Eadem" ("The Month," January, 1904; continued in "The Catholic World," August, 1905), in favour of a much simpler view more consonant with facts and with unsophisticated tradition; one which neither implicitly degrades the present to exalt the past, nor degrades the past to exalt the present; which finds the type of ecclesiastical growth neither in a dialectical, nor in a mechanical, nor in a physiological process, but in processes of the same order as itself. For as we cannot explain physiology by mechanism, so neither social and religious processes by physiology.

LEX CREDENDI

PART I

"THE SPIRIT OF CHRIST"

I
THE SCOPE

THE purpose of the present writer's book called "Lex Orandi" was to show that the doctrinal system of Christianity is the result of the attempt to fix and formulate the implications of the Church's spiritual life; that "vitality" is the test of truth, not in Newman's sense of the phrase, not as though mere persistence and survival were enough, but in the sense that a belief which universally and persistently fosters growth in the spirit of Christ is not only pragmatically true, but is proved to be, in some symbolic way, representative of that world of ultra-reality in accommodation to which our spiritual life consists.

It was necessary in such an undertaking to assume that the "spirit of Christ" and the "spiritual life" were values familiar to all, or easily determinable; for a criterion must be something better known or more easily knowable than that to which it is applied. The concrete is prior to the abstract; the masterworks of art are prior to art-theories and art-rules; and if we test art-works by these rules and theories, yet we will accept no theory that would condemn what are admittedly master-works of art. Here is a circle, but not a vicious circle. The master-works are the supreme criterion; theories and rules are but instruments for the application of that criterion. Master-works are above criticism; at times they break up all our theories and systems. If we measure them by our rules, it is rather to test and verify those rules; to bring them back to their source. So, too, we "try the spirits," we test the conduct of Christians immediately by the teachings of Christianity, ultimately by the life of Christ, by the spirit of Christ, which itself is the criterion of sound teaching. The doctrine of the Church is avowedly nothing more than an unfolding of the implications of the spirit of Christ, of the life of Jesus. That life necessarily implied certain conceptions of God and of man and of their relations one to another.

To these conceptions the spirit of Christianity owes its distinct and unique character. Without any unfolding of these implications it is possible for those whose spirit is akin to Christ's to feel at once the harmony or discord between other lives and His life, other ways and His way; to make His Way and Life a direct criterion of false and true. But such criticism is too subjective, too uncertain, too unverifiable to be of general service in the corporate life of the Church. In due limits the art and theory of any sort of life is necessary to its general advancement among men—necessary for the protection and proper application of those standards which are furnished by the creations of genius, by the works of God or of Nature. We judge the lives of ordinary Christians by Christian teaching; but when this teaching itself is in question we test it by the admitted or classical standards of Christian life; we turn to Christ, whose life is, in a sense, a divine revelation, an implicit "depositum fidei," and to the greater Saints, whose lives are, so to say, authentic developments of His, authentic manifestations of the same spirit. Teachings which harmonize with these sacred lives, which foster and further that spirit in others, express the true implications of Christianity.

It is the purpose of these paragraphs to consider, not the teachings of Christianity, but Christ; not the implications of His life, but the life itself; in other words, to give more definite meaning and content to the term, "the spirit of Christ."

As before (in "Lex Orandi") there was an inevitable tendency to force the interpretations of theology in the interests of pragmatism, so here there may be a like danger of unconsciously shaping our presentment of the spirit of Christ in the interests of theology. Even were our present purpose apologetic and not purely practical, it would be in the best interest of apologetic to lay aside all theological prepossession, and to allow the theme to work itself out freely, confident that the result will, on the whole, verify our religious teaching.

We must not come to the master-works as critics with our art-theories; but as learners, with an open mind. Doubtless we shall learn from them what thousands have learned before us. But we shall learn it ourselves, and possess it in a new way.

II
THE METHOD

"Let it therefore be our chief study," says à Kempis, "to meditate upon the life of Jesus Christ. The teaching of Christ excels all the teachings of the saints, and had one His spirit one would find therein the Hidden Manna." Some rudimentary sympathy with the spirit of Christ is the indispensable condition of understanding the Gospel. We cannot construct an idea out of nothing; the beginnings, the germ, must be already within. If there be but a rudiment of Christliness within us we can develop this germ into a more perfect image or presentment of Christ. And to understand Christ's spirit is nothing else but thus to reproduce it in ourselves. In order to hear and recognize His voice it is needful to have heard it before, to be His sheep already—as we all are, unless conscience be wholly extinct in us.

But there are other subsidiary conditions independent of our spirit and moral character. "How shall they hear without a preacher?" It is needful that the word should enter the ear and the mind before it can enter the heart and spirit. Every aid that learning offers us to ascertain the exact mental value of Christ's teaching, the precise sense which it conveyed to His hearers (were these good or evil, friendly or hostile), is of inestimable value. For though its spirit is incommunicable save to the sympathetic, yet the vehicle of the spirit, the bare sense, is communicable to all equally, and of that vehicle every fragment and particular is vocal and eloquent to those that have ears to hear.

We must then always strive to determine as exactly as possible what sense our Lord's words conveyed and were intended by Him to convey to His hearers, to Peter, Andrew, and John, or to the scribes and Pharisees. For He did not speak *in vacuo* nor use some absolute or ideal language. A musician's performance is always limited by the range and possibilities of the instrument before him; the speaker or word-artist must work within the limits of the language and ideas of those whom he addresses. The mentality, the education of the Galilean crowds fixed the range of that instrument through which Christ had to convey the eternal truth of the Gospel. He could give only what they could receive. Hence we must in all cases first ask ourselves: "What did these words mean for Peter, Andrew, James, and John?" before we go on to ask: "What do they mean for us? How would He have spoken to us had He lived in our day, so as to convey to us the same spiritual and eternal values?"

And we must remember to distinguish carefully between that spiritual value and the words and ideas which are its vehicle. When we translate the primitive forms of religious thought and language into our modern forms we do so at some risk—the risk of spilling the precious wine of the word in pouring it from one vessel into another. Though we must not give to the primitive vessel the sacredness of its content, yet it has a derived and secondary sacredness of its own as being the first and divinely chosen vehicle of revelation. Thus, to come to our present preoccupation, before we attempt to determine what "the spirit of Christ" should mean for us, we must ask ourselves what it meant for the Apostles and for the Christians of the Apostolic age. For, rightly understood, Apostolicity is the criterion of Christian truth; not in the sense, e.g. that Peter's notion of a "spirit" is to be a norm and fetter for all subsequent metaphysics and psychology, but in the sense that it was the vehicle of religious and moral values which we must take care to secure when we venture to substitute our own philosophy for his. Apostolic teaching is classical as the most perfect manifestation of the Christian spirit, albeit in a most imperfect medium. There is more truth, more spirit, in a rude draft of a Michelangelo, were it but of a single limb, than in the finished perfection of an Andrea del Sarto.

It is not in the rudeness, but in the spirit, of Apostolic religious thought that we are to look for the criterion of Christian truth.

There is little doubt as to what a "spirit" meant for the Apostles, when they spoke of men being possessed by evil spirits or being filled with the Holy Spirit, or when our Lord promised that His Spirit would abide with them. In the simple philosophy of earlier times, whenever a man's mind or tongue or limbs or faculties seemed to be wrested from his own control and made the instrument of an intelligence other than his own, whether better or worse, this effect was ascribed to the locally and materially conceived entrance into him of a spirit, i.e. of a principle akin to that which normally animates and controls our bodies when we are alive and leaves them when we are dead. We can see now that in many ways this first effort of philosophy to explain the normal and supernormal phenomena of our life is necessarily anthropomorphic and childish; but though to some degree we may seem to have corrected its crudities we should be less pardonably childish ourselves did we fancy that our deeper philosophizings had entirely escaped from the necessary flaw of anthropomorphism, and even materialism, which must always vitiate our efforts to represent things spiritual.

Our philosophical notion of a spirit may be less imperfect than that of the Apostles: we may legitimately refuse to fetter our metaphysics and psychology to those of earlier times or to make an idol of the ancient vessel out of reverence to its content; but neither may we make an idol of the modern, nor flatter ourselves as having attained finality and ultimate perfection.

It is with the moral and religious effects of these possessions and inspirations that religion is directly concerned, and not with the metaphysical nature of the agency to which they are due or with the mechanism of its operation. It is concerned with the presence or absence of certain spiritual gifts and qualities. Where there are love, joy, peace, and the other gifts and fruits of Grace, religion speaks of a spirit of holiness entering in and making its abode in the soul; taking control of it; raising it to a supernatural mode of life. Where, on the contrary, the normal power of self-determination is shattered; where some vice or passion seizes the reins of government, usurps the throne of reason, divides the house of the soul against itself—there it speaks of the presence of a tempter, or an evil spirit. Christian art and imagination pictures such exits, entrances, presences, as local and material, and the symbolism is practically serviceable and convenient. So far as it is thus serviceable it is true to the purposes of religion; but to its philosophical truth, religion as such is indifferent. If, however, because religion speaks with practical truth, of an unclean spirit going out of man, as out of a house, and wandering in dry places, or because sacred art represents the exit as that of a winged mannikin from the mouth of the possessed, we give philosophic truth to such images, we are literally superstitious, for we cover with the mantle of religion what is no part of religion.

III
THE MEANING OF "SPIRIT"

In modern language the term "spirit" is used in a moral sense as well as in a psychic or metaphysical sense. It stands for a certain complexus of ideas and sentiments; for the character or quality of a man's thought and feeling. These have been conceived as rooted in and manifesting the occult nature of the spirit of which they are the phenomena; of the "I" which thinks and feels; and the name "spirit" has been transferred from that which thinks and feels to the thought and feeling in which it makes its hidden character known. That every spirit was unique, the only possible one of its kind, was a point of mediæval philosophy to which perhaps we owe our modern use of the word "spirit" as designating what is distinctive and individually characteristic of each personality; as being the equivalent of personality in this moral sense. For "personality," too, has been transferred from the metaphysical substance to its manifestation in life, thought, sentiment, and conduct. Here at all events it is undeniable that no two personalities or spirits are alike; for each is the resultant of its own history, of a sum-total of experiences whereof no one can ever be matched precisely in all its inwardness and outwardness.

When in this modern sense we speak of "the spirit of Christ" or of "the spirit of Holiness" we do not directly mean what the Apostles meant by the Holy Ghost; and at first sight it might seem somewhat sophistical to work with ambiguous terms as though they were univocal, and to read a modern sense into ancient language. And this would be so were our interest philosophic and not religious; were we quoting Apostolic writings as authorities in metaphysics rather than as authorities in Christianity; were we studying the vessel rather than its content. We have no direct metaphysical insight into the nature of the human spirit or of the Divine Spirit. They are known to us only through and in their effects, through the thoughts, feelings, utterances, and actions of man, whereof some are attributed to man's own spirit, others to the influence of good or evil spirits over man. Since therefore spirits are known to us only in their manifestations, and interest us only as the sources of these manifestations, and so far as we (like the Apostles) are interested in religion and not in philosophy, we are not false to Apostolic thought if we prescind from the metaphysical connotation of the word "spirit," and confine ourselves to its religious and moral values. Here we must be at one with primitive oracles; there we may, and to some extent must, differ from them. The religious meaning (e.g.) of the descent of the Holy Ghost is the same for us and for them; yet the precise psychology of the event may be differently estimated by us; whether more or less imperfectly, who shall say?

If then we speak of "the spirit of Holiness" rather than of "the Holy Spirit" as guiding the Church into all knowledge, we are only uttering the same religious truth with greater precision; we are fixing our attention on the "formal aspect" under which the Holy Spirit acts as our guide, and withdrawing it from the religiously irrelevant conception of the metaphysical nature and mode of that operation. When we say that the spirit of Fra Angelico has exercised a guiding influence in art, we do not deny that this influence derives in some mysterious way from the metaphysical principle of his being; but for artists, such a consideration is irrelevant; for them, in this connexion, his "spirit" means its manifestation in certain effects and productions whose guiding influence in art is explicable artistically.

It is only in the life and utterances of Christ that His human spirit is revealed to us; nay, we have no other revelation even of that Divine Spirit of which He possessed the plenitude. In that life of His, therefore, we have the classical or regulative manifestation of the Spirit by which all other manifestations are to be tried and measured. For all its limits of time, place, occasion, language, tradition, that life alone is a pure utterance of the Divine Spirit; the finitude, the limitation is solely on the part of the vehicle. Given such material to work upon, it could not have been more divinely shaped and mastered. The greater the limitations within which it works, the more fully is the creative power of the artist revealed. It was in the language and conceptions of Galilean fishermen, not in those of modern culture, that the Word took flesh. Is it so evident that these latter had been a better vehicle of revelation? It may seem so to the intellectualist; but not to those who see in Christianity a revelation of the spirit, not of the letter; who look to its religious, not to its philosophical values.

What precisely do we mean by the *spirit* of Christ, the spirit of Christianity; by knowing Christ no longer after the flesh but after the spirit?

A man's spirit is doubtless something that is betrayed or manifested in his conduct, words, and actions; but is felt to be distinct from these embodiments and, as it were, their animating principle. It is not literally resident in them, but in their author. When we say it is *manifested* in them, we mean that there is a certain mode and manner, to be distinguished from the substance, of such utterances which betray the intention, the mind, the personality, the sentiment from which they proceed. In substance, and abstracting from mode and manner, they might be the product of any spirit, but taken concretely they could be the product only of one.

Different playwrights or artists will treat the very same theme with an infinite difference of treatment. In that difference is revealed their spirit and personality. We feel, moreover, that this spirit is in some sense an unique quality; that if it be the resultant of simply innumerable and incalculable factors, yet it is not merely their sum, but rather an indivisible point whither rays of influence converge from all quarters, making it what it is, and no other. Again, we distinguish the faultless finished work that results from calculation, understanding, and practice, from the faulty, but far higher results of one who has "caught the spirit" of the idea to be realized; who is guided by that spirit rather than by any rule. This points to the spirit as being primarily a sense, feeling, sentiment, or instinct—not necessarily, or even possibly, a *blind* feeling; but one whose determining perceptions and experiences are too infinitely complex to admit of any sort of analysis or statement. When used as the equivalent of one's whole "personality," and not only with reference to certain particular interests, it is that abiding massive sentiment or state of feeling which is determined by the totality of our experience past and present, forgotten and conscious.

Though betrayed in the words and conduct to which it gives birth, yet a "spirit" is not directly communicable; it cannot be formulated. The signs of anger seen in another are not the feeling itself. Only in the measure that I have felt anger myself and uttered it in these signs is it possible for another to communicate his anger to me.

And so of his spirit; only so far as my own spirit is potentially (and to some extent actually) like his, do his utterances shape my sentiment into conformity with his. Hence, Christ is made to say: " My sheep hear My voice"; i.e. only Christians can hear Christ. As the soul is wholly in every part of the body—to speak scholastically—or as the organism is potentially in each of its constitutive cells, and can, in some cases, be renewed from any one of them, so the whole of a man's spirit is incarnate in his every deliberate word and action, and might be inferred therefrom by a comprehensive and all-penetrating kindred spirit. But in point of fact it is only by the accumulative effect of a great variety of impressions and manifestations, correcting and supplementing one another, that we can gradually approximate to that precise and unique quality of sentiment which belongs to a personality other than one's own.

Hence, according to our degree of potential spiritual kinship, it is possible for us to divine the spirit of Jesus revealed in the scattered utterances and reminiscences preserved to us in the Gospels; to feel and enter into the affection and sentiment of which they are the expression; and thus indirectly to apprehend that view of life, of time and eternity, by which the said spirit and affection are determined. It should be possible for one fully possessed by the spirit of Christ to divine, by a sort of tact or instinct, how He spoke and acted or would have spoken and acted under given circumstances. And such a portrayal might be a far truer revelation of His mind and personality than the shreds and scraps of biographical evidence that have come down to us. Historical fiction may be truer to inward reality than historical fact.

We must allow considerable importance to a man's philosophy as both shaping and revealing his spirit; yet so far as it is imposed on him by tradition it rather hides than reveals it. So far as he reacts against its influence, shapes it, and gives it a personal impress or style, we have a revelation of his distinctive quality of mind. But even were he to elaborate a whole system for himself from ground to roof, yet this self-analysis may be wholly inaccurate, must be at best inadequate, abstract, formal; for, as we have said, a spirit cannot be formulated; what I feel in the face of my world, in the face of all my experience past and present, can no more be uttered than that experience itself; it can at most be hinted or symbolized, and interpreted by those who have felt more or less the same. What I *feel* about life may be much truer than what I think or say about it—even to myself, i.e. it may be the product of a truer, though of an obscure and inexpressible intuition.

If "the pure in heart shall see God," it may be because the feeling toward life of unspoilt hearts may enwrap depths of philosophic truth which will never find utterance in system.

For if we assume, as surely we may, that the world itself is the symbolic self-utterance of the Divine Spirit, then it is to those spirits most attuned to the Divine that the inward sense of that utterance will be most fully revealed. Others will apprehend the bare sign, the dead letter, the mere physics or physiology of the matter, for lack of that inward kinship with the Divine Artist which He Himself works in the souls that do not resist His ingress.

Whatever the philosophical or theological deficiencies of the language in which Christ had to speak to the fishermen of Galilee, yet they could not hinder the revelation of His spirit, of that feeling with which the purest of all human hearts reverberated to the love of the Divine Heart symbolized in the work of the Divine Hands—a feeling that enwrapped a philosophy which no categories shall ever compass; a love kindled by a glance from that Love which is the Root and Reason of all things.

No theological construction of Christianity, however faithful and laborious, could ever guide our life so surely in accordance with the ultimate truth of things as could even a little measure of the spirit of Christ—of His feeling toward life, toward God and man and all creation. That is the true *Gnosis*, of which it might be said, "Ye have an unction from the Holy One and ye know all things"—not merely in the way of practical knowledge, but potentially in the way of theoretical knowledge, in the sense that the implications of that feeling, could they be unravelled, would open the very heart of Reality to our understanding.

IV

CHRIST'S SPIRIT AS FEELING

If it is convenient and suggestive to speak of the spirit of Christ as a feeling or sentiment, we must be all the more careful to enter an emphatic caveat against the sentimentalism, or emotionalism rightly or wrongly associated with the name of Schleiermacher. Intellectualism, Voluntarism, Sentimentalism, are three fallacies that have played a great part in the history of Christianity. Each is usually the result of a reaction against the extravagances of one or both of the others.

All assume in common that the spirit-life may be portioned out into three quite separable departments—knowing, willing, and feeling—and that some one of these must reign supreme over the other two; and each claims this supremacy for itself. Yet this division is a mere work of abstraction for the convenience of speech and reflex thought. There is not a movement of the spirit in which knowledge, feeling, and will do not interpenetrate. When this is clearly recognized, it matters little from which of the three sides we approach the study of the spirit-life, since each entails the other two, and if we grasp one we grasp all. If however it is forgotten, it matters very little which part we treat as supreme and independent, the result can only be extravagant, abstract, unreal, and its nemesis will be an equally extravagant reaction in favour of one or other of the neglected claimants for supremacy. Religion does not consist in knowing; it does not consist in feeling; it does not consist in willing and doing, nor is it a sum or addition of all three; but it is a life, an operation in which the mind can view now under one, now under another of these aspects. It is not possible to feel with Christ, unless we think and will with Him, nor to think with Him, unless we feel with Him, for the spirit-life is one and indivisible.

Yet "thinking" may mean two things; and for this reason it is more convenient for our present purpose to view the spirit of Christ as "feeling." Every feeling implies some apprehension or knowledge which explains it. But this implied apprehension is one thing, and the explicit account we give of it to ourselves or to others is another. It can never equal or exhaust, it can easily misinterpret and pervert the concrete mass of perceptions on which the feeling is founded, or rather, with which it is interpenetrated and interwoven. The reasons we give to ourselves or to others of our likes and dislikes, of our attractions and aversions, of our passions and emotions, are a small part, if any, of the multitudinous reasons which we cannot give and yet which are acting upon us. It is of these latter, not of the former, that we speak when we say that the spirit and inward life of Christ may be viewed indifferently as knowledge, feeling, or will. It is the total response of His spiritual being to the Divine Reality by which it is encompassed and in which it is rooted; the response of a soul so absolutely pure and translucent as to be able to see down to those all but fathomless depths where it springs from the heart of eternity; a response that is at once vision, feeling, and will; "none afore or after the other; none greater or less than the other."

We need then to distinguish between Christ's vision and the expression of that vision; the latter being but a rude sketch or suggestion of the former in terms and conception familiar to the fishermen of Galilee.

If then we prefer to speak of the spirit of Christ as "feeling," we are not sentimentalists, for we recognize that this feeling is also vision, that it is a principle of discrimination, a guide to truth.

The influence of feeling upon reason, for good or evil, is a commonplace. It is possible just because every feeling involves a judgment, and this judgment of feeling may conflict with the judgment of reason. In this sense feelings are true or false. I like a man or dislike him without reason or against my reason. My feeling (i.e. my implicit judgment) may be true and the judgment of my reason false or inadequate. Sometimes rightly, sometimes wrongly, according to the quality and clearness of the feeling, we correct the judgment of reason and arrange our beliefs so as to justify and explain our feelings. In this sense St. Thomas Aquinas speaks of faith as a sort of instinctive discernment or feeling whereby even the unlettered can scent out heresy through the sympathy of spirit with spirit. It may not be true of all the faithful distributively, but it is true of them collectively, true of the Church in whom the faith of her members is focussed and purified. From all this we can understand how the spirit of Christ, though something akin to a feeling or instinct, acts as a principle of doctrinal discrimination and development. More commonly we speak of this guidance, with reference to its supernatural and metaphysical causation, as effected by the Holy Ghost working in the souls of men. But here we view it as the orderly development of the effect of that working of the Holy Ghost in the soul of Christ, as the development of "the spirit of Christ" in the moral sense of the term spirit; as controlled by Christ's spirit in the way that a legitimate growth is controlled by its germ. The truth, the intensity, the depth, the purity of Christ's spirit, that is, of His vision, feeling, will all in one, was such as to make it indeed the Light of the World. To unravel the implications of that Love fully and rightly, were any human language or thought-system adequate to the purpose, would be to lay bare the fulness of Divine Truth, moral and religious, to reveal all the mysteries of the Kingdom of God. For from the vision of these things, that Love was kindled, that spirit was created. Here was a feeling the truth of whose judgments might stand as sovereign criterion of the judgments of formal reason:

> And like a man in wrath, the Heart
> Stood up and answered: 'I have felt.'

It was not for our Divine Saviour to invent so contradictory and unserviceable a thing as a final and absolute philosophy and language, and therein to embody exhaustively the inexhaustible meaning of His Love. His revelation was no divine "Summa Theologica" written with the finger of God; it was His own Spirit of Love which He bequeathed, with all its implications, to His disciples. The theology implied in that Love, the notions about God and man and their relations on which it was fed, were brought to expression but gradually, as occasion demanded, through conflict with uncongenial doctrinal systems. Thus we can see the loving spirit of Christ correcting and reinterpreting all that was harsh and unlovely in the religious teaching to which the Apostles had been familiar. Similarly, throughout the ages, it acts in the same manner upon the doctrinal materials presented to its criticism, and thus slowly its own implications find fuller and more adequate expression.

Proximately it may often seem to be theological ingenuity that settles points of doctrine; but ultimately it is the verdict of the Saints, i.e. of those who possess some measure of the discerning spirit of Christ, the true *regula fidei*. Well may the Church honour and worship the sacred books of the Gospel with her most solemn ceremonial, with lighted torch, and waving censer, and tender cadence, and reverential kiss. For these are the *fontes Salvatoris*, the salutary wells, from which, time and again, she has drawn living water in her days of spiritual drought and famine. " Back to Christ, back to the Gospels,' has ever been the watchword of Salvation in such seasons; back, that is, to the classical, normative manifestation of that spirit by which all other spirits have to be tried and criticized; back to the very thoughts and words of the Apostles, not as to a final rule of thought and speech, but as to the rude vehicle and embodiment of the first, fullest, and supremely authentic manifestation of the spirit of Christ.

Every great forward movement in the Church's life has been a sort of Gospel renaissance, a return to some forgotten or perverted point of Apostolic Christianity. So with the reëdition of the Gospel of poverty and simplicity through St. Francis of Assisi. So, too, when the reforming Council of Trent insisted

on the importance of the reading and preaching of
the Mass-Gospels to the people. Again it was through
meditation on the Gospels that Ignatius Loyola hoped
to revive and sustain the spirit of Christ in the
face of renascent paganism. It is on the same staff
that the present Pope leans for support in his work
of reform; and perhaps while his other efforts are
thwarted in a thousand ways, the little society of
St. Geronimo with its cheap gospel-texts may be the
mouse that is to gnaw through the network of complications. Be this as it may, enough has been said
to show that the life, the prayer-life, the spirit-life,
whose furtherance is one of the great criterions of
doctrinal truth, is not something vague, subjective,
elusive; that it is the Life of Christ, the spirit of
Christ as revealed to us in the Gospels. Its closer
determination is not arbitrary, but will lead us to
a study of those priceless records.

V

CHRIST "ACCORDING TO THE SPIRIT"

To know Christ no longer after the flesh but after
the spirit (not perhaps in the Pauline metaphysical
sense, but more in that ethical sense of which his
conception was a symbol) means to believe in Him,
hope in Him, love Him as the embodiment of the
Divine Will; of the cause for which He lived and
died; of the Gospel of the Kingdom of God. This
is the love He cares about when He asks men to
leave all "for My sake *and the Gospel's.*" The holy
women loved Him, and the disciples for the most
part loved Him with a human love; but of His

spirit, of the governing enthusiasm of His life, they had no realization, and hence they could have no adequate sympathy with it;—nay, at times they were jealous of it because it detached Him from all lower ties and affections with which they fain would have bound Him to themselves. It was another Self they cared for than that which He had made His own by the constitutive act of His Will. "Get thee behind Me, Satan!"—so He slights and repulses the warm-hearted but purely human love of Peter. And from the woman who clung to His feet to keep Him on earth for ever He shook Himself free: "Hold Me not, for I have not yet ascended to My Father"; and to His parents He says: "Why did you seek Me? Did you not know that I must be about My Father's business?" It was to His spirit, or to Himself only as embodying that spirit, that He strove to win their love and loyalty. The fire with which He burned and which He came to kindle was an enthusiasm for certain ends and certain principles, for all that was summed up in the conception of the kingship of God in men's hearts, of the Divine Will realized on earth as in heaven. This fire, or enthusiasm, is "Christ according to the spirit" or "the spirit of Christ." It is, indeed, the work of God immanent in and pervading the workings of man's spirit, and trying to bring forth His image therein. To be permanently and absolutely the voluntary instrument of this Divine enthusiasm; to be so completely and perfectly wielded by God's Will that the action and effect must be called simply Divine, all separate personality being merged indistinguishably in that of the Infinite Spirit; to be subject to it as the hand or foot is to its owner—is the moral manifestation of that mysterious hypostatic union which entitles Jesus to be called the Son of God in an unique and incommunicable sense.

This is the ethical and religious value which finds theological expression in the doctrine of the Incarnation,—a doctrine which recognizes the infinite gulf that divides the ideal from its closest conceivable approximation.

"Christ according to the Spirit" is another name for God as effecting that ideal in the human nature of Jesus and making it purely an instrument of the Divine operation; and as striving to effect an approximation to that ideal in each one of us.

"For My sake *and the Gospel's*"—this, then, is the key to true "devotion," to that devotional spirit whose furtherance is the end and therefore the criterion of doctrinal truth. In his book on "The Characteristics of True Devotion," Abbé Grou adds his voice to that of all the great masters of the spiritual life in warning us not only of the possibility, but of the existence of spurious devotion to Christ. It is not enough to love Christ in any way; we must love Him precisely as the representative and embodiment of the cause for which He lived and died, the cause of the Gospel, of the Kingdom of God. "It is the spirit that giveth life; the flesh profiteth nothing": it is in the love of Christ's spirit, not in that of His flesh that Eternal Life is found. In our own experience what is more distressing, more disappointing, than to be loved and admired for qualities which we know we do not possess; or for those which we do not value, or even dislike in ourselves; and, on the contrary, to fail to attract others to what we believe to be best in ourselves, or to interest them in our deepest interests? We are overwhelmed with affection that pleases us as little as would a complimentary letter intended for some one else but mistakenly directed to ourselves. For all our seeming friends, we stand unloved and alone. To a great extent this was the lot of Christ upon earth. He was loved, but mostly with a human love and "according to the flesh," not with the love that meant a likeness of spirit. Is it otherwise now? Alas, they are not so many who love Him at all, that we can well afford to stop and criticize their love and ask whether it be according to the flesh or according to the spirit; whether it be a love of the Christ of the Gospel or of some other Christ of their own fabrication or fancy. Yet ask we must; since identity of name is no guarantee for identity of notion, and it is at least possible and probable that our Christ may be largely fashioned in our own image and likeness. In the Christ of the Gospels the Church gives us an objective criterion of all these subjective Christs of our own. In the measure that the lines of that portraiture puzzle and bewilder us, that they lack life, unity, and coherence, we may suspect our own spirit of being at fault; but when we find them falling together, growing intelligible, taking life and warmth and strength, then we have a sort of inductive assurance that our spirit is shaping rightly; that it has the clue to the labyrinth. Speaking of the visions of St. Gertrude and Blessed

Margaret Mary, a devout Catholic lady recently remarked to a priest: "They tell us about our Lord, and without them one would know nothing of Him." "Do you ever read the Gospels?" asked the priest. "Oh no, they are *so* dry." Here, no doubt, there was devotion to Christ of a sort, but hardly of the healthiest sort; and one feels that it was fed, not by the Gospel spirit in the said visions which alone constitutes their substantial value, but by what is accidental in them and secondary, by their poetic appeal to the emotions, to the æsthetic need; that it was not worth much more than would be a delight in the physical beauty of the Sacred Humanity. The question is therefore not only: "Do I love Christ?" but also: "Why do I love Him? under what aspect?"

Here as elsewhere mischief comes from a onesided view of the nature of spirit-life; from making sentiment everything, or conduct everything, or mysticism everything; from forgetting that they are all sterilized when divorced from one another. If Christ does not evoke and satisfy all our spiritual needs, there is surely a flaw in our devotion somewhere; it cannot be the Christ of the Gospel, the spirit of Christ, which draws us.

VI

SENTIMENTALISM

There is plainly a very undesirable sort of sentimentalism which systematically builds up such an image of Christ as will appeal most sensibly to the emotions of the devotee, to love and pity; which uses the belief in His Godhead to legitimate what else would be the idolatrous worship of created beauty, of "the fairest among the sons of men." It does not rest altogether in the exterior. No truly æsthetic emotion does that. But being so largely æsthetic, it is very dependent on the imaginable as on the medium in union with which alone such beauty is revealed. It must gaze up into the eyes of Christ; it must hear His voice, read His smile, feel His embrace, cling to His feet. It envies those who knew Him "according to the flesh," when He walked and talked with His disciples in Galilee:

> How I wish that His hand had been placed on my head,
> That His arm had been thrown around me,
> And that I might have heard His kind voice when He said,
> 'Let the little ones come unto Me.'

Surely a most inevitable and natural wish. Which of us would not wish to have seen the great and wise of old, or is not interested in those features of their personality which have nothing to do with their greatness and wisdom, yet which gain a value for us as associated with them?

Sentimentalism does not lie in valuing these dependent and associated interests, but in forgetting the principal interest which is the source of their value; in concentrating upon them. Some will be thrilled by a visit to Stratford-on-Avon who have never thought or felt with Shakespeare in their lives. It is equally possible to have a tender love of every feature of Christ's Sacred Humanity, and yet never to have thought or felt with the spirit of Christ, and to find the Gospels "dry." For indeed they cater but little for sentimentalism and leave us ignorant of those thousand details about which such devotion is curious. Love of this kind is no doubt the love of One who is believed to be God; but is it the love of God, the love of that which is Divine in Him? The nursing of such an affection by such means—that is, by the selection just of such traits, real or imagined, as will build up a Christ in the interests of devout feeling—must necessarily lead to a continual falsification of the Christ of the Gospel. He came to "show us the Father,"—as it were, in the mirror of His own life and spirit—so that between our love of the reflex and our love of the Father there might be no difference of motive, but that we might come to the Father through Him.

As I have said, it seems a poor service to religion to criticize any sort of devotion to Christ, seeing it is all too scarce a commodity. Yet perhaps the same criticism that makes us cast aside certain sorts as spurious, unhealthy, or decadent, may show us a great deal more of the best sort in quite unexpected quarters; in many of Tertullian's *animae naturaliter Christianae* who, never having heard of Christ, are Christians unawares. "All who have ever lived by the Word," says Justin, "were Christians even though they were reputed to be atheists, as was Socrates among the Greeks." Moreover, since all direct cultivation of feeling for its own sake leads to the corruption and impoverishment of feeling, it can be nothing but a service to devotion to point out this danger and abuse. We have allowed that sentiment is an element in true devotion; that we cannot love Christ fully unless it be with every part of our soul;

but we have defined sentimentalism to be the error which makes feeling the whole or the principal part of devotion.

All this being clearly understood, there are certain facts that we ought to face bravely and frankly, for they have much to do with the present impotence of Christianity.

It is not without reason and justice that we speak of woman as "the devout sex": "Ora pro devoto femineo sexu," says the anthem of Our Lady. It is sometimes said that women are by temperament more religious than men. This I think seems true, partly because our religion has been so much shaped by women that as a fact it has been largely adapted to their temperament. I doubt if the same impression would obtain in the East, where men think meanly of woman's spiritual gifts and give her a secondary, if any place at all, in the Kingdom of Heaven. That the catalogued saints of the Church are predominantly men does not really alter the fact that, in proclaiming the spiritual equality of woman with man, Christianity has made it possible for her to play a preponderating part, not (overtly) in the government, but in the religious life and devotion of the Church. For naturally she has more leisure, and, in some ways, more need for the services of religion. Be the reasons what they may, the fact remains that, from the first, devotion to Christ has been mostly the devotion of women, religious or others; that the Christ which it has created is to some extent a woman's creation, and since demand determines supply, the male preachers and exponents of that devotion have rather yielded to, than resisted or corrected, the tendency to feminize the presentment. "Men drawn by women," says Sir Leslie Stephen,[1] "even by the ablest, are never quite of the masculine gender. They may indeed be admirable portraits, but still portraits drawn from the outside." This merely means that likeness and sympathy are the condition and measure of understanding. In the fulness of Christ's humanity there is more than all that fulfils the two ideals of manhood, the woman's and the man's; but these ideals are different and it is the woman's ideal that prevails most widely in the pulpit, in religious art, in devotional language and literature. And the result is that the Christ so presented fails to appeal to, if it does not somewhat repel, men of the masculine type, to whom action means more and sentiment less than it does to the feminine type. Were we to make a holocaust of nine-tenths of our pious pictures and images, it might be symbolic of the reform needed in this matter. We owe much, no doubt, to the visions of St. Bridget, St. Gertrude, B. Margaret Mary, Sister Emmerich, and others; but on the whole the spiritual gain has been for women rather than for men; and we cannot help suspecting that male visionaries—if there had been truly such—would have presented the "perfect man" to us under a somewhat "drier" aspect, in which case we might have been spared the coarse and blasphemous revolt of the Nietzsche school in favour of the so-called "Superman" (*Uebermensch*) and against the supposed Christian ideal of diluted manhood.

[1] "George Eliot," p. 74.

The remedy against all sentimentalism of this sort is to be sought in a return to the Gospels, in an endeavour to get at the integral spirit of Christ as it lives for us there, whole and concrete, not split up into factors. Only when we understand and feel with that which was the central interest of His life, that sovereign end with which He identified himself, which was the core of His moral personality and spirit; only when we love that in Him to which He most wanted to win our love, and for which alone He cared to be loved,—only then is our loving interest in all other things that concern Him a pure and wholly acceptable sentiment, an outflow or redundancy of that central and substantial devotion to the Divinity revealed in Him. "Weep not for Me," He says to the women on His way to Calvary, "but weep for yourselves and your children." Their tears were those of womanly pity for the outward and obvious aspects of the tragedy, but of its inwardness they knew nothing. Their love was for Him, yet not for His central Self or Spirit, which they could not understand. We may stand by His Cross, enter by force of keen imagination into all His pangs and tortures; we may mourn, as a friend for a friend, or as a woman over her first-born, for the torn and bleeding God, and yet lack the true key to the meaning of His Passion and waste ourselves in sentimentality. The true sentiment of pity must flow not from any sort of love of Him who suffers, but from that sort which He most desires. We do not mean to disparage the lesser love, or the sentiment which it genders; but, as we have said, to emphasize the danger of resting in it, of cultivating it as an end in itself, of confounding with the love of God *as God*, the love of One who *is* God. The genuine and discerning love of Christ " according to the spirit" will necessarily foster and perfect our sentiment and deliver us from all danger of sentimentalism.

VII
" MYSTICALITY "

If, on the whole, sentimentalism is a devotion to Christ "after the flesh"—a shaft which misses what is the very heart and centre of the matter and sticks fast in what is merely adjacent—there is another sort of devotion more spiritual, more intellectual, which is equally ill-aimed and leads to analogous perversions for analogous reasons: a sort of false mysticism which, for convenience, we may call "mysticality." As before, the error comes from separating aspects that should be organically inseparable. The integral Christ satisfies at once our emotional, our moral, and our mystical needs. A Christ that satisfies but one or two of these needs is a divided, a perverted Christ; and the spirituality fed on such a Christ is a false spirituality, either unpractical or heartless or rationalistic or dreamy or metaphysical.

At all times man has experienced certain feelings of awe and reverence in the face of the immensities and eternities in the midst of which he and his little world are afloat. He is ever straining his eyes through the nearer gloom that deepens away into that impenetrable darkness whence all things come and whither they return; ever seeking to understand and adapt himself to that All which lies beyond and explains the nearer world of his clear vision. Every sense of contact with that mysterious Beyond lifts him above earth and out of himself; and though his native materialism of thought and desire drag him down again and again, yet his restlessness and discontent with earth are incurable. Were it but a need of his intellect, we might call it his "metaphysical need"; but it is primarily a need of his heart which earth is too small to satisfy, and, as such, let us call it his "mystical need,"—the need whose perverse cultivation leads to "mysticality."

In old-world thought the connexion between religion and morality was obscure. Sometimes religion was but a department of morality,—our duty toward God; at other times morality was, in comparison with observances and forms of worship, only a subordinate part of religion—the religious sense fed itself almost exclusively on the thought of the Beyond without reference to the moral life. It was Christianity with its conception of God as subsistent righteousness, its recognition of the voice of conscience as the voice of God, that first revealed the two interests—the religious and the moral—as identical, and thereby gave a mystical depth to morality, and a moral earnestness to religion, and brought this world and the Beyond, and our lives in reference to both, into a coherent unity. Abortive attempts in the direction of this identification are traceable in the Orphic mysteries; but neither the ethical nor the religious elements were there sufficiently purified to reveal the full secret of their sympathy and to admit of their final and permanent synthesis. In the Hellenic world, in which Gentile Christianity first took shape and with whose spirit the spirit of Christ entered into a relation of mutual permeation, struggling to leaven it and transform it to its own nature, religion in its highest and, to Christianity, most congenial developments was in the main mysticism, not to say "mysticality." Its purest though subsequent culmination is associated with the name of the neo-Platonist Plotinus. However over-speculative and intellectualist, however extravagant in its dualistic contempt of the body as the antagonist rather than the complement of the spirit, there was much in this mysticism for Christianity to work upon. At first sight there might seem to be little kinship between a religion of the crowds, of the poor and simple, a religion altogether practical and concrete, and one that was so largely philosophical and abstract, the monopoly of a small intellectual aristocracy, whose ideal attainment was mental ecstasy rather than moral devotion. Yet this pursuit of intellectual ecstasy, this audacious effort to push behind the veil of the visible and to live a superhuman life entailed a contempt of this world and the flesh, an aspiration after higher things, a hunger and thirst after righteousness with which Christianity could not but sympathize, —Christianity with its own doctrine of "the two ways," of the flesh and the spirit, of death and life; with its call from earth to heaven; with its crowds of Saints, Martyrs, and Confessors who lived the exalted life that philosophers but dreamed of.

This "way of life" was to a great extent common

ground; but whereas with the Greek it was merely the condition of the life of intellectual contemplation and ecstasy, something secondary and deduced, with the Christian it was primary, the very substance of his religion, of eternal life. For him Christ was the Truth in an altogether practical sense; "the Way, the Truth, and the Life," were synonyms. And so far his doctrine of the Cross was "to the Greeks foolishness." They wanted the philosophy of the matter. They knew by experience that contemplative ecstasy depended partly on asceticism and the mortification of the flesh; that this disordering of the body was the condition of those unnatural mental states which they assumed to be supernatural. But the Christian had no such motive for his mortification and unworldliness, which were dictated merely by the exigencies of absolute self-devotion to the service of God and man, or else by a belief in a speedy world-catastrophe that cancelled a number of otherwise rational human interests.

Yet the Christian's indifference to theory and philosophy could not hinder the fact that his way of life and his spirit necessarily involved a theory of God and man, of time and eternity, of here and hereafter,—a theory that could not but become explicit as soon as reflection set to work. In so far as "the Way" was common to Christian and philosopher, the theory of that Way was bound to have many points of contact on both sides; and it was just here— namely, in regard to its intellectual implications— that Christianity blended with Hellenic mysticism, each giving to and receiving from the other. For the sake of the Greek, Christianity now became interested in its own implicit theology and mysticism and brought them to expression in the language of philosophy. But while acknowledging the due claims of the mystical and intellectual interest, Christianity fought hard against the excesses of intellectualism and "mysticality." If religion was not all conduct, so neither was it all mysticism. Already in the New Testament, in the writings of St. John and St. Paul, we see this accommodation of Christianity and Hellenism in process; on one side, the full acknowledgment of the mystical interest, on the other, the emphatic protest against its usurpations. For St. John, Love is the Truth, the true Gnosis, the true Light, the true Life. For St. Paul Charity, the spirit of Christ, is above all mystical gifts and graces, above visions and ecstasies and prophecies and miracles and intuitions. These have their place, but it is a secondary and dependent one. Life is something far greater and fuller.

The Greek then was inclined to be more interested in Christology than in Christ; in the metaphysics of the Spirit than in the fruits of the Spirit; in the theory of life than in living. And his devotion was apt to run into mysticality; to feed itself too exclusively on mysteries, to revel in the twilight outside the little sphere of our clear intelligence and even to tempt the further darkness. When St. John tells him that Jesus is the *Logos*, the Reason, the Truth, he at once acknowledges the rights of his mysticism and repudiates its usurpations: "You seek a false *Logos* for your mind alone: here is the true *Logos* for your heart as well. You seek a false light that shines only for an intellectual *élite:* here is the true Light that enlighteneth every man that cometh into the world." Let the Greek look first to the plenitude of the spirit-life, to the Kingdom of God and His righteousness, and all his mystical needs would be inclusively satisfied. For, the mysterious relationship of Christ to the Father and through the Father to the world and mankind, was wrapped up and implicated in the Way of Life which He taught us, and was the secret of the inexhaustible depth that distinguished it from mere moralism or practicality. Not only to unwrap it, but to separate it from the living whole, to make it the central and even the sole interest of the Gospel, this was the danger for Greek Christianity which had to be met by a system of concessions and limitations.

If we are told that "God is a spirit," this is doubtless a metaphysical affirmation, a negation of materialistic notions of the Divine Substance which would confine the Deity to houses made with hands, to Jerusalem or to Mount Gerizim. But the real interest of the Evangelist is not in the metaphysical statement, but in the ethical and practical truth of which it is the implication: "They that worship Him must worship Him in spirit and in truth." For him the rule of prayer and life is the rule of doctrine and belief. Let the life and the worship be purified from materialism, and doctrinal purity will look after itself. His own interest, unlike the Greek's, was less in the metaphysical spirituality of God's nature than in the ethical manifestations of that nature in man, in the spirit of holiness, in the fruits and gifts of the Spirit, in grace and charity. God is a "spirit" because God is Love. And so, too, while not forbidding the Greek to exercise his intellect and feed his religious awe on the mystery of Christ's metaphysical relationship to the Father and to the world, the Gospel calls him back continually to the great life-interest on which this mere mind-interest is wholly dependent, back to the life and the ethical spirit of Christ as the manifestation of the Father's love and goodness, as the Word or Expression of the Divine character and will in human terms; as a truth to be lived and not merely contemplated. "Mysticality" just inverts this order of dependence. It concentrates the soul wholly or principally on the metaphysics of Christ's being, and not on that aspect of it on which He wishes us chiefly to concentrate ourselves,—not on His life, His spirit, His way. It leads us to adore Him as the incarnation of the First Cause, as the Alpha and Omega of creation, and feed our mystic appetite on our contact through Him with the Eternal and the Infinite. So far as it stops here it makes us descend from the fulness of Christianity, with its identification of Godhead with Goodness, to the level of those earlier religions for which God was Power rather than Righteousness.

There is a latent mysticism involved in the Christian "Way of Life" and organically inseparable from it. If we separate it from that living unity, we tear it from its root and source of vitality, and are compelled to nourish it from the turbid streams of philosophical speculation. We end with what is a devotion to Christ no doubt; and in one sense a devotion to Christ "after the spirit" rather than "after the flesh"; and so far it is an advance on mere sentimentalism. But if we take "spirit" in the religious and moral sense, and not in the metaphysical sense, then we must reckon "mysticality" to be a devotion to Christ "after the flesh"; for it is not a devotion to Him formally as to the embodiment of the Gospel, of the Divine Will, of the Cause of God on earth; nor does it spring from such a devotion, but rests in the metaphysical mystery of His being as though this were the substance of His teaching.

Devotion of this kind will perhaps find food in a onesided reading of the Fourth Gospel and of parts of St. Paul. But it will find the Synoptics "dry"; yet in truth its Christ is as little the Christ of St. John as it is the Christ of St. Mark.

The correction for mysticality, as for sentimentality, is to be found in a return to the integral spirit of Jesus that still lives for us in the evangelical records, a spirit that satisfies all our needs and delivers us from the false pieties that are fostered by its dismemberment. He who dissolves Christ is anti-Christ.

VIII
"PRACTICALITY"

The third error, which I will call Practicality, is so much the more dangerous because of its resemblance to the truth. Nevertheless it is as much a dividing of Christ and of His spirit as the other two. It is a far more prevalent error in these days of practical, utilitarian, common-sense Christianity, and in a workshop atmosphere little congenial either to sentiment or to mysticism. It has not a more plausible or able exponent than Matthew Arnold. He partitions life between conduct, science, and art,—a division which is, at root, almost identical with that which we are following. Conduct, he insists with somewhat wearisome iteration, occupies exactly three-quarters of life; art and science each one-eighth. Three-quarters of conduct, *plus* one-eighth of art, *plus* one-eighth of science, equals life. Right conduct is righteousness. Instead of God we are given a "Not-Ourselves that makes for righteousness." This "Not-Ourselves" is, then, concerned about three-quarters of our spirit-life, about conduct. It is indifferent to the remaining quarter,—to science and art; it does not make for truth or for the beautiful.

Now this is to divide the spirit with a hatchet; and it is hard to conceive how one to whom intellectual and artistic truth meant so much, could have so sundered these interests from that of righteousness or failed to see their organic and indissoluble connexion. A less thoughtful person, however, might easily be excused. For we certainly see that very good people are often quite indifferent to intellectual and æsthetic truth; while the devotees of these latter are often as indifferent to truth of conduct. But Matthew Arnold ought to have known that these several indifferences, if complete and deliberate, are eventually fatal to the favoured interest. As a fact, they are never complete and deliberate; no good man says: "Knowledge does not matter"; "Art does not matter"; nor is any artist or thinker wholly indifferent to conduct. It is a question of imperfect balance, of undue emphasis.

Instead of "the Not-Ourselves that makes for righteousness" (i.e. for right conduct), let us rather say "that makes for truth—truth in conduct, truth in thought, truth in feeling"—that is, for the truth of the whole spirit-life of man, for its progressive correspondence to the life of the Eternal Spirit. By the time we have made this amendment, we have got back from Matthew Arnold's divinity to that of the Fourth Gospel: "God is a spirit, and they that worship Him must worship Him in spirit and in truth." We have given to the "Not-Ourselves" the character of that which it "makes for,"—the plenitude and perfection of spirit-life. We cannot give it less.

Conduct is not three-quarters, but the whole of life; for there is a conduct of the mind and a conduct of the feelings. Conduct, thought, and feeling are each the whole of life,—three dimensions of the same thing; there is no "human act," no movement of the spirit-life, into which they do not all enter.

When we say, "Faith without works is dead," we mean that it is not really faith at all; that intuition and feeling necessarily embody themselves in will; that the spirit cannot really apprehend a situation without taking some practical attitude toward it. So, too, works without faith are dead,—the mere corpse of conduct. If they are true works, true actions of the spirit, they are necessarily an expression of faith,—of intuition and feeling; they are faith viewed from another end.

What favours "practicality" is the fact that we only see men's good works, but do not see their faith; that for social utility and beneficence it matters more (immediately, not ultimately) what men do than what they feel or mean. Thus, by a false abstraction, conduct comes to be cut off from the unity and fulness of spirit-life; Christ comes to be regarded as the incarnation of right conduct in this narrow sense; and the value is laid on the outward manifestation rather than on the immanent spiritual reality of His righteousness. We have already said that in Christianity for the first time the interests of man's mystical sense (for which earlier types of religion catered almost exclusively) and those of his moral sense were clearly recognized as identical, inasmuch as the Will of God and Righteousness and Truth and Love were proclaimed to be the same thing. We said that what we called "mysticality," or false mysticism, partly ignored this identity and was so far a reversion to a lower type of religion. It is equally plain that "practicality" also ignores the said identity; that it is blind to the mystical depth of Righteousness and of Divine Love, to their latent implications of a world of supernatural reality beyond the little sphere of our clear vision, and separated from it by that band of twilight in which the mystic loves to linger. "Practicality" is right in affirming the great and primary importance of conduct as a test of spiritual reality, as a criterion of faith and doctrine. The "fruits" to which Christ appealed were "good works" that men could *see*. But there is a mere surface seeing, and there is a spiritual discernment that leaps from the outward expression to its true inward significance, that sees the faith through and in the works.

It is with this vision that we must come to the Gospels if we would get at the spirit of Christ in its fulness and solidity, and not merely recognize one or other of its dimensions. It is, however, through the conduct-dimension that we are to get at the other two, and so to grasp the whole. Passing thus from the conduct-aspect to the fulness of that spirit-life of which it is a partial manifestation, we shall escape from that mere "moralism" or "practicality" which Newman has so justly criticized is his three essays on "Rationalism in Religion." On the other hand, we shall be saved from a false, abstract, merely philosophical mysticism or "mysticality," if we contemplate the being of Christ not apart from, but only in and through, the life in which He has revealed it to us; if we feed our mystical appetite solely on the mysteries latent and implied in His spirit and in His redeeming love. Thus, too, we shall find the measure and criterion of healthy religious feeling or sentiment, and protect ourselves against a fruitless sentimentality.

In fine, we shall learn to love in Christ just what He wanted us to love; to feel about Him just what He wanted us to feel; to know about Him just what He wanted us to know. Our Christ will not be a Christ of our own, a maimed or divided Christ, a Christ "after the flesh"; but the true Christ, Christ "after the spirit."

IX
"CARITAS DEI"

Sentimentality, Mysticality, Practicality,—none of them exists pure and unalloyed in the soul of any worshipper and follower of Christ. Each stands for an exaggeration of one of the elements of true devotion and a consequent enfeeblement of the other elements. The right adjustment or blending of all three is called, in the New Testament, "Love" or "Charity"; that Charity which St. Paul says is a "more excellent way," a greater gift than all other gifts or sharings of the spirit of Christ, because it includes and overpasses them all, and because without it, and except as flowing from it, they are nothing worth; better than the understanding of mysteries and of all knowledge; better than prophecy and miracle-working and speaking with tongues; better than giving all one's goods to feed the poor, or giving one's body to be burned. This Charity is "shed abroad in our hearts" by the Spirit of Holiness which is given to us; nay, it is that same Holy Spirit dwelling in us; it is God Himself, for "God is Charity."

Here, indeed, is food for mysticism; for we are dealing with relationships between the divine and human which necessarily defy, and so will always defy, definition or accurate expression. If we seize one-half of the truth, we have to let go the other; and whether we hold them together or separate them we fall into some contradiction. We are safest when we leave metaphysics, with its problems of sameness and otherness; and instead of considering its subject or agent, simply consider the life itself, the process, the love. This process of living and loving we can clearly characterize as divine or human, as supernatural or natural, according as man lends or refuses himself to be the perfect instrument of the Divine Will, the flawless mirror of the Divine Goodness—though we know that "instruments" and "mirrors" must be utterly inadequate symbols of the ineffable metaphysical relationship between God and the soul.

Unfortunately these words "Love" and "Charity" have been "soiled with all ignoble use." The former is overloaded with sentimental and mystical associations; the latter has lost all depth and tenderness through the loveless deeds that are done in its name, and stands at best for the business of philanthropy. No name will safeguard the idea, for the meanings of words are continually corrupted. Even if, to make sure, we call it "Christliness" or the "spirit of Christ," this will not avail, unless our conception of Christ's spirit be kept sane and well balanced by a persistent pondering of the Gospels; for we are all inclined to some sort of characteristic onesidedness in our idea of Christ; we shape Him, directly or indirectly, according to our own image and likeness.

If then we want to determine what that spiritual life is whose development and increase in ourselves and others is the end and chief criterion of religious truth, we must turn to the Gospels, we must study it in Him "of whose fulness we have all received and grace for grace." All the apparatus of religious institutions and teachings is but the channel through which the living water flows from His soul into ours to produce in us the fruits of the same spirit. The apparatus is justified if the results correspond.

It will be reasonably objected that "the eye sees only what it brings with itself the power of seeing"; that each will read his own Christ first into the Gospels and then out of them. In a book called "Jesus von Nazareth im XIX Jahrhundert," H. Weinel has shown us how variously and contradictorily the Gospel has been read in the last century; how many conflicting causes, philosophies, and interests have claimed Jesus for their master and exponent.

Against such scepticism, which would rob the Gospels of all objective meaning, let it be noticed that the diversity of the said views is founded rather on the actual sayings and doings of Christ than on the inward spirit embodied in them, about which there is little explicit interest; that they are reached by reasoning from them rather than by feeling with them; by looking to their logical consequences rather than to their inspiration; by taking them as isolated oracles rather than as diverse manifestations of one and the same spirit. This is a fallacy of "literalism" to which we shall return presently.

Secondly, the Gospel is not of "private interpretation" any more than are the great master-works of art. In these the uneducated eye or ear discerns little; praises and blames the wrong things; misses the unity, the spirit, of the whole. Yet this is no plea for scepticism and relativity. The artistic truth is there, and those who would reach it must study to correct their faulty vision till the common judgment of the discerning becomes their own, not by forced obedience to authority, but by a personal conviction "of sin and of righteousness," i.e. by an awakening from darkness to light, from "dryness" to refreshment. The first impressions of the Gospel will be as various and different as the minds impressed. But we can trust to its power as an instrument of spiritual education; the longer it is pondered, the more it will shape those various minds to its own truth and bring them toward a perfect agreement with one another. We do not come to the Gospels spiritually blind or wholly untaught. We have imbibed something of the Christian tradition around us; we know what others have found there before us; and now we come to verify this collective experience of others for ourselves, to make it from a hearsay into a living experience of our own. As long as we find the study "dry," the fault is in ourselves. For this we have the assurance of those millions to whom it has been "a fount of water springing up unto everlasting life."

But we should certainly expose ourselves to grave misunderstanding did we not say a word against what we may call the fallacy of "New Testament Christianity." When we say "Back to the Gospels," we do not mean back to a phase of Christianity that cannot and ought not ever to return; what we do mean we shall consider in a separate section.

X
"NEW TESTAMENT CHRISTIANITY"

So-called "New Testament Christianity" is purely and blindly reactionary; it is a denial of all flexibility and vitality in the religion of Christ. Its perfect realization were only possible if we could miraculously change ourselves back into the mental and social conditions of Palestine two thousand years ago. No one pretends that the perfect imitation of Christ requires that we should all be carpenters, or that we should all live at Nazareth; yet this is really implied in the principle of so-called New Testament Christianity. Plainly, it is the spirit of Christ which we have to imitate, though the matter upon which, and the conditions under which, we have to work are wholly different from His. For the discerning, the spirit of the master-artist lives whole and entire in the least and rudest of his efforts, and can be gathered still more easily from a collection and comparison of them all. But to canonize the vehicle together with the spirit which it conveys, to copy his works slavishly and mechanically, were to make a tyrant of a teacher, and to bring the spirit under the bondage of the letter.

What we have to study in the New Testament is the spirit of Christ at work upon matters which often concern us very indirectly or not at all. The religious errors He combated were not those of our day; the scribes, lawyers, Pharisees, and Sadducees, with all their controversies and causes, are only analogously represented in modern times. The more closely and critically they are studied in the light of the past, the more evident is the measureless gulf that divides their mind and sentiment from ours. We have for so long read the Jewish Scriptures through our Gentile glasses that we falsely credit ourselves with understanding the Judaism of Christ's day far more than is really possible. The needs and social condition of the crowds to which our Lord ministered were so unlike those of our crowds that a mechanical imitation of His methods is full of danger. And so in other matters. This is largely forgotten by those who turn to the Gospels for guidance in intellectual, social, and political matters, forgetting that most of what are called "questions of the day" could not have been formulated or understood in Judæa two thousand years ago; that surface-analogies, however striking, are profoundly dangerous and misleading. The Christianity of the New Testament, the first embodiment in which the spirit of Christ manifested itself, was necessarily shaped and framed either in accordance with, or in opposition to, conditions which have vanished for ever. To deny the equal right of later and fuller manifestations, to hold us back to the first as to an iron rule, would be to nail Christ hand and foot to another Cross, to bury Him in the tomb of the past without hope of resurrection.

What makes New Testament Christianity in some sense classical and normative is that it exemplifies for us the working of Christ's spirit in its purest form and at its greatest intensity,—albeit under conditions that have largely ceased to obtain. However different the matter subjected to its influence, yet the tendencies of that spirit, the mode of treatment, are always the same. It is through the modification produced by the Gospel-spirit in its environment, through its selections, repulsions, attractions, that its character is disclosed to us, and its implications are made explicit. To have expressed all those inexhaustible implications at once and abruptly; to have anticipated the final results of an endless process of unfolding; to have made an absolute revelation in an absolute language without reference to the mental and moral capacity of any age or people, would have been utterly futile, had it not also been intrinsically impossible.

In a sense the Holy Spirit, the Spirit of Christ, was itself the Revelation, the *depositum fidei;* nor is the manner in which doctrines, systems, and institutions lie latent and implicit in a spirit or sentiment at all unfamiliar to us. We commonly reprove a man for letting his feeling bias his judgment or blindly control his conduct. That it does so, means that the feeling is full of implicit judgments and practical consequences that are first brought to light by their conflict with the judgments of reason. My dislike of a man requires for its justification that a certain prejudiced reading of his character and conduct should be true; that my action toward him should be hostile; and so forth. If this is a disadvantage when my feeling is wrong and untrue, it is a great advantage when my feeling is right and true, when it is in touch with fact and reality, when it is the feeling of a spirit that is rightly and healthily adjusted in relation to God and man. Thus the "charity that thinketh no evil" is a divine and true feeling, and the construction it puts on things and the direction it gives to conduct (seemingly, but not really, *a priori*) is far truer than the dictates of mere reason and calculation; for it is begotten by the immediate contact of the soul with God, who is the root of all reality.

And of this charity, Christ's spirit is the plenitude; and what we see in the Gospels is just this spirit of Christ working everywhere in its own interests; in its own justification; broadening what was narrow; deepening what was shallow; softening what was harsh; raising what was low in the religious, moral, and social ideas and institutions of our Lord's own day and people. We see it selecting, attracting, repelling, according to its own exigencies; slowly leavening Judaism and transforming it to a vehicle of self-expression; moulding its conceptions, its language, its symbolism, its traditions to its own use and service.

Notably in St. Paul the implications of this spirit were brought to light in their opposition to the uncatholic and exclusive elements of Judaism, whose limits of adaptability were thus at last recognized as too narrow to admit of a full and free expression of Christianity. With the speedy accretion of Gentile multitudes to the little flock of Christianized Jews, the leavening process was for the moment thrown back to begin again on a vastly larger scale and in an entirely different, in many ways more congenial, medium. For the strictly Judaic elements of New

Testament Christianity, even in its Pauline form, the Græco-Roman religion, or religions, of the Empire had little affinity or power of assimilation; but they had much of their own that lent itself to a richer and more flexible manifestation of the spirit of Christ and of all that distinguished Christianity from Judaism. It was the spirit, rather than the body, of New Testament Christianity that passed over to the Gentiles, and began there its work of leavening that great syncretism of all the religions of the Empire into a vast catholic, world-embracing Church. Much that was a scandal to the Jew was congenial to the Gentile. The notions of a plurality of Divine persons; of an incarnate God; of a theotokos; of a deity slain and risen; of sacraments and mysteries; of asceticism, world-flight, and consecrated virginity,—all these notions and the catholic idea itself were familiar to him. The Christian spirit had only to correct and spiritualize what was gross and superstitious in these conceptions, to tolerate what was indifferent, to supplement and utilize what was good. And this process by which the spirit of Christ slowly shapes for itself a body and organism out of the materials offered to it by the philosophies, beliefs, institutions, traditions of those who come under its influence is unending. If its New Testament embodiment is in some sense its most vigorous and purest expression, yet it is far from being its complete expression. For this we must wait till the last page of its history is written. And through those pages there are scattered other manifestations of it which have become in a secondary sense classical and universally authoritative for all subsequent times, —institutions and developments which have been proved and accepted by the experience of all as genuine "explicitations" of the spirit. It is the whole body of these that constitutes Catholic Christianity,—a body whose parts are not all, for our minds, dialectically linked together or deducible from one another, however lawfully we may, *post factum*, strive to detect such a unity. Their connexion is that of the various works of some great master-artist which in all their diversity of theme and circumstance exhibit and transmit one and the same spirit, and are valued solely on that account.

We see then at once the truth and the fallacy of "New Testament Christianity"; and how false and thin a conception of Christ he would have who, without distinguishing the spirit from its embodiment, should take the religion of the Synoptics or even of St. John or St. Paul as the sole and only legitimate expression of Christianity to be slavishly imitated by all future ages, to be a fetter on all progress and lawful variation. This has been the mistake of all puritanic reforms inside and outside the Church whose cry was "Back to the Gospel" or "to the Bible." Certainly, if we compare St. Francis of Assisi with a typical Puritan or Bible-Christian, we shall find that the latter thinks, speaks, and conducts himself generally (or a least strives to do so) much more in accordance with the New Testament embodiment of Christianity; but who does not feel that, for all the palpable differences that exist between the external religion of the first and the thirteenth centuries, St. Francis' spirit is immeasurably truer to the spirit of Him whose consciousness of Divine Sonship lit up the whole world for Him with a joy that no sorrow could quench, whose delight was to be with the lilies of the field, with the birds of the air, with little children and with the sons of men? In one case we have a conscious imitation of a past manifestation of the spirit, in the other a new and original manifestation of the same spirit; the Puritan copies an ancient masterpiece, St. Francis is inspired by it to yield new results.

New Testament Christianity errs in attempting to identify the Gospel exclusively with one of its infinite manifestations; in forgetting that the spirit of Christ is "one, manifold, subtle, more active than all active things, and reaching everywhere because of its purity."

If this is an error, yet it is perhaps a greater error to speak of a "Christianity pure and simple," as if we could separate the spirit from each and all of its embodiments and study it apart. For we do not know it in itself at all, but only in its workings; nor can we apprehend it or speak of it except in terms of its effects. Therefore what we must study in the Gospels is precisely the conflict between Christ and His surroundings; between His spirit of love and the ideas, beliefs, traditions, and institutions of His people and country. We must try to see just where these were congenial and were offensive to His spirit; to notice the way in which He modified, interpreted, corrected, or supplemented them. In a word, we must watch His spirit in movement and at work;

and not simply contemplate the work done as if it were a theme for mechanical copying. What we want to get at is the Master's secret, His creative power.

XI

HOLINESS AND TRUTH

To realize that the Spirit of God guides the Church first into holiness and through holiness to truth; that the Holy Ghost precisely as holy, and as the author of holiness, is the Spirit of Truth, is to cut away the ground of one of the commonest attacks on the whole idea of doctrinal authority. When we say, "*first* holiness and *then* truth," we are speaking of the truth of explicit understanding which is attained by after-reflection on that truth which is always implicit in holiness and quite inseparable from it; we mean the truth of the *Credo* already latent from the first, but only gradually drawn forth from the *Pater noster*, —the *verité pensée* as distinct from the *verité vécue*.

We hold that the Church is "infallible" in doctrine, but we deny that she is impeccable in conduct; we affirm that Holiness is one of her notes; and we explain it by saying: "She teaches a holy doctrine and offers to all the means of holiness and is distinguished by the eminent holiness of her children."

Were we speaking of the Invisible Church, that "Sancta Ecclesia Catholica" which is identical with the "Communio Sanctorum," with the assembly of the Just in heaven and of the Just on earth, whether inside or outside the pale, we should need no qualification. That Church is holy, simply because *all* its members are holy. But plainly we speak of the

Visible Church, the sacrament, symbol, and instrument of the Invisible, the bodily organism through which its life is normally and principally manifested and sustained; we speak of that field in which tares and wheat grow together till the harvest; of the net containing all manner of fishes, good and bad; of the Church which moral corruption has assailed at all times with varying degrees of success; whose very life, like that of our own bodies, is a continual fight with death, an endless process of self-repair and self-reform which may not be interrupted without disaster. The notion of a *visible* institution whose members shall all be saints is little short of a contradiction, since sanctity is a secret of the heart known to God alone. From the days of Montanus down, all attempts to realize that notion have issued in like results. Pharisaic pride, hypocrisy, and imposture are inevitable wherever external status is supposed to be a sure guarantee of inward worth, or of anything more than a belief in an ideal. If we call ourselves Christians, it should rather be to condemn ourselves than to approve ourselves.

The Visible Church is the vessel that contains the leaven and the dough, and so brings the latter under the influence of the former. To separate the one from the other, to assess their ever-varying proportions, is impossible. To call oneself a Catholic, only means that one freely subjects oneself to be leavened by the secret influences of the living part of the Visible Church,—for there is always a dead part and a living, however difficult it be to distinguish them clearly.

The attack above mentioned is founded on the manifest ethical corruption to which the Visible Church is subject. Is it likely, we are asked, that Christ, who certainly did not guarantee ethical infallibility or sinlessness, should have guaranteed doctrinal infallibility to the Church and its officials? Is not the former a far deeper need? She is His Vicar and representative; why does she not represent Him in this? It was by example that He Himself taught and guided men; not by doctrinal decisions: "Learn of Me," He says, not because I am a theologian, but "because I am meek and lowly of heart"; and to His Apostles He says: "Let your light so shine before men, that they may see your good works." It was as an example of life that He was the Light of the world, a City set on a hill, a Good Shepherd who goes before the sheep; and the Apostles were to carry on the same work by the same method. This surely is what is meant by the promise of an abiding Spirit of Holiness, and by saying: "As the living Father hath sent Me, so send I you"; "He that heareth you heareth Me." His disciples are not the learned scholars of a rabbi, but those who "take up their cross and follow Him." When He prays that His disciples "may all be one, that the world may believe that Thou hast sent Me," the unity is surely that of which He says: "Hereby shall all men know that you are My disciples, if you love one another." And when we study the history of the Apostles (who, moreover, theologians tell us, were confirmed in grace and sinless), surely their teaching and guidance were all of this same practical experimental kind: "Be ye followers of me, as I am of Christ Jesus." Their authority, like their Master's, was entirely spiritual, appealing to the heart and affections, not coercing the mind or the will; it was not that of "the rulers of the nations" (divine in its way and in due measure), but His who though He was the greatest became as the least; who recognized that, of its very nature, the spirit may be drawn but cannot be forced. Had the successors of the Apostles, or even of Peter alone, been confirmed in grace; had men always been able to turn to the Church or the Bishop of the City of Rome for an infallible pattern of Christliness in life and conduct, surely we should have had miraculous evidence that Christ was with us always, even to the end of the world; we should have been well content to leave doctrines alone in their implicit state and to follow our Shepherd trustingly and unquestioningly. For doctrine is but the theory of eternal life to aid us to conceive what we do not behold; but if it is there before our eyes, who needs the doctrine?

All this would be unanswerable, were the Visible Church intended to be a "Collective Christ" in attainment and not merely in aim and aspiration; were she a finished work, and not an endless growth toward an ideal. Being what she is, a mixed multitude of good and evil, living and dead, we have no more right to look for Christ in her average life than in her lowest; we must seek Him in her best, and in those acts in which she turns round upon herself to criticize and reform herself according to the dictates of her conscience, i.e. according to the Spirit of Holiness which animates her living members.

The Spirit of Truth is with her just because the Spirit of Holiness is with her. In neither case is the measure quantitative or numerical. Had she but one saint, the leaven would still be there in the midst of her. But she has multitudes of such, known and unknown, of various levels and degrees of Charity; and it is in these collectively that the Spirit of Truth and Holiness dwells and spreads its leavening influence to the savourless mass around.

As average Catholic holiness is not the holiness of Christ, so neither is average Catholic truth or doctrine the truth of Christ. Is there a single mind, even among doctors of theology, wholly free from ignorance, misunderstanding, and superstition in religious matters? Catholic truth, explicit to some extent in the minds of the learned, lies implicit in all its fulness in the hearts and spiritual lives of the holiest members of the Church, and all that the official teachers of the Church can do is to mediate between the highest and lowest levels and make these latter benefit by the spiritual riches of the former.

We say rightly that the decisions of councils and popes are more or less determined by the Holy Ghost. As a fact of the metaphysical order we hold this on faith; the mode of causation is as hidden from us as is the nature of the two agencies involved, —the divine spirit and the human. But the effects of this mysterious operation are given to our observation, and we can study their connexion and interdependence. Thus history shows us to some extent the process by which this Divine guidance of the Church is effected; it shows us how the really fruitful and lasting decisions have been called forth and shaped by the influence of the saints; by considerations of the practical bearings of dogma on the spiritual life rather than by speculative considerations. The guide whom councils practically and ultimately follow is the Holy Spirit as active in the living members of the Church. The spiritual life and needs of these is really the determining agency; these, all unconsciously, are the guides and teachers of their brethren. For, avowedly, nothing new can ever be defined, but only that which is already implied in the Christian life. The Pope is in theory no irresponsible absolutist who can define what he likes, who can make truth and unmake it. He is but the interpreter of a law written by the Holy Ghost in the hearts of the saints. He is bound by this living book. The Christian revelation, the *depositum fidei*, is the spirit of Christ with all its implications. If we say that that revelation culminated in Christ, it is because no sanctity can be greater than His. If we say the Church can develop that revelation, but not add to it, it is because the saints only share and "explicate," each in some special way, the fulness of Christ's sanctity. The particular form or symbol in which the implications of Charity or Grace find expression is but the vehicle of the Spirit which is expressed; its truthfulness is its greater congeniality to that Spirit as contrasted with some other expression which it excludes and denies. So far then as the Church is guided purely by the Holy Ghost in her doctrinal decisions, her eye is fixed on the spiritual life of the faithful, and in the light of that interest she shapes her verdict with the sort of infallibility that belongs to every spiritual instinct. There are rare crises in the Church's history when the mystical life of her living members is intensified and concentrated and silently exerts an irresistible pressure on the minds of her official teachers, forcing them to act and directing their action in its own interest. However scholastic and theological the reasonings may be by which their decisions are professedly justified, yet the true motive and directive power is always the Holy Ghost, always some practical need of the spiritual life. To take the most unfavourable case, the condemnation of Galileo may have been ultimately in-inspired not by any alleged speculative interest of science or astronomy or even of exegesis, but by a just fear of the spiritual disaster that would result from a sudden revolution of theological thought for which the general mind was as yet wholly unprepared. Scientifically the argument from practical inconveniences is inadmissible, but "pastorally" it should be respected within due limits. For if our deepest faith tells us that the interests of life and truth must be at root identical, we may resist a tenet which seems hostile to life until its evidence actually coerces our assent; and then the same faith will assure us that its hostility to life is only apparent. As long as it is still disputable, science and religion will each solve the question in its own interest. Thus, instead of dismissing it as a complete mistake, we ought to distinguish between the religious and the scientific values of the condemnation of Galileo, as of every other doctrinal decision of the same weight and solemnity. What the religious instinct implicitly affirmed was only that fundamental religious truth which seemed to be implicitly denied by Galileo's affirmation. And thus of all judgments so far as they are truly forced from the Church under pressure of the mystical life of her living members; they are all protective of that life and of the one deep truth implicit therein.

Thus the Visible Church is infallible in doctrine because she is, and in the same measure that she is, holy in life. As sin and frailty abound among her members, so also ignorance, superstition, and doctrinal error of all sorts,—wheat and tares; good fish and bad. It is to her living members, to those who are animated by the Spirit of Holiness and Truth, that we must look for that mystical Christ who is with her all days, even to the end of the world. They collectively are the seat of her spiritual vitality; from them the leaven of truth and holiness is communicated to those around. To bring both sorts together in one receptacle, to mediate between them, to distribute the strength and light and riches of the few among the many, is the very end and aim of the ecclesiastical organism, with its institutions, its official teachers and rulers,—itself the creation of that Spirit, and guided by that Spirit.

XII

THE PERFECTION OF MANHOOD

We know that our religion is true because it fosters in us the true life, the life of Christ, the spirit of charity. We turn to our Lord Himself, as He still lives for us in the Gospels, to study that life in its highest and most classical manifestation; and we shall find that charity is neither "Sentimentality," nor "Mysticality," nor "Practicality," but the ideal of Perfect Manhood in its fullest and richest development.

The perfection of manhood is the perfection of a spiritual being made to be the mirror of the divine perfection. "He that hath seen Me hath seen the Father. How then sayest thou, Show us the Father?" From the very nature and necessity of our thought we can only "realize" and deal with a spirit like, but indefinitely more perfect than, our own. We *know* that God is infinitely more than this; but for us that "more," that surplus, is an outer darkness. Christ's perfect humanity has revealed to us as much of the Father as we can ever imaginatively "realize," love, or deal with ; He has translated the divine life into terms of human life: "The Word was made flesh and dwelt among us." We know now by revelation (for Christ *is* that revelation) that all which is best in man, and immeasurably more, is found in God:

> So through the thunder comes a human voice
> Saying : 'O heart I made, a heart beats here!
> Face My hands fashioned, see it in Myself !
> Thou hast no power, nor may'st conceive of Mine,
> But Love I gave thee, with Myself to love,
> And thou must love Me who have died for thee.'

For all practical purposes of life and religion, our God is in human form, and that form is primarily the form of Christ ; secondarily and dependently, that of His brethren of all ages and nations. Through Him "we have access to the Father"; "No man cometh to the Father but by Me."

To-day a revolt from Christianity has raised up a new standard, a new ideal,—the *Uebermensch*, the Superman or "More-than-man." Let us look patiently and sympathetically at this new doctrine and see whether it may not contain, as every heresy does, some perversion of a too long neglected truth, some angry reaction against excesses in a contrary direction, against perversions of the Christian ideal of perfect manhood for which Christians are in some measure responsible.

It has recently been contended [1] that the only type of manhood which now commands respect in Western civilization, or lives effectually as a goal of moral endeavour and a potent factor of progress, is neither Christian nor Greek, but "Gothic." It is not the Saint, with his mystical other-worldliness, his womanish tenderness, patience, and compassion; his asceticism and mortification; nor is it the "phronimos," with his absolute reasonableness, his cold, statuesque perfection of conduct; but it is the military or "Gothic" type, with its ideal of chivalry and honour as the great duty of man. The others still linger on men's lips: this alone rules in their hearts. So far as there is truth in the contention, it points to the fact that the Christian type is either misapprehended or misrepresented, or both; for the true ideal of perfect manhood is a salt, a moral and social antiseptic, that can never possibly lose its

[1] "Christian, Greek, or Goth?" by H. Garrod: the "Hibbert Journal," April, 1905.

savor or fail to appeal strongly to the taste and appetite of the healthiest and most vigorous. It shows that the prevalent notion of Christliness is out of touch with life in some way or another.

It is to a revolt of Nietszche against his former guide and master Schopenhauer, that we owe this new fetich-ideal of the " More-than-man," more kin to the " Gothic " than to the Greek or Christian type. Schopenhauer's pessimism, his conviction of the total and irremediable badness of life, made him the violent foe of Jewish optimism, and even of Christianity so far as it was saturated with Judaism. It threw him into sympathy with Buddhism, with its antagonism to that "will to live" which it views as the cause of all the sorrow and suffering entailed by the struggle for existence and by the impulse of self-assertion, self-preservation, self-propagation. Obviously the whole inspiration of this sad decadent philosophy is sympathy with the pain of the entire sentient world, a pain that preponderates immeasurably over the meagre sum of pleasures in the opposite scale. If Christ had the merit of being in sympathy with all this pain, yet He was no pessimist ; for He taught that this sorrow might be turned into joy, that it was light and momentary compared with the weight of glory to be revealed. Schopenhauer accepted Christ's condemnation of the present world as hopelessly wretched ; and welcomed the great example of pity and sympathy and world-flight; but with His doctrine of Hope he would have nothing to do.

However innocuous in the motionless East, the decadent and demoralizing tendencies of this pessimism in our progressive Western civilization soon made themselves felt to healthier and more vigorous instincts than Schopenhauer's. With Nietzsche the reaction became vocal. " Away with this puling pessimism and its corollary of enervating pity! Back, not to Judaism, but to a frankly pagan belief in the worth of what this life has to offer, a belief destroyed by sickly over-reflection, by mystical peerings through the clouds into dream-land. Let us take life simply as unquestioning children take it, as it was taken in the childhood of humanity. Let us trust in the rude self-asserting instincts of unsophisticated Nature. She knows what she is about. Through the struggle of each for himself, through the survival of the strongest, the elimination of the weakest, she has shaped the beast into the man; let her alone and she will shape the man into the More-than-man. Pity for the feeble and maimed only weakens them and weakens ourselves; it multiplies the image of suffering by a series of mirrors and gives it an intensity and importance of which healthy savages know nothing. Still more, all the energy, thought, and time that go to the service of compassion are worse than wasted; they but secure the survival and multiplication of those whom Nature's kind ruthlessness would eliminate, and they do so at the expense, and to the exclusion, of the hardier type. It is to self-worship that we owe the heroes, the strong men, the strong peoples, of history: to the instinct that bids a man give the fullest possible play to all his energies, and forbids him to emasculate or mortify his manhood in any way; or to stand aside to let the weaker pass.

Away with the Saint and his otherworld; with the "phronimos" and his pedantry of virtue and self-restraint, and let the Strong Man come to the front once more. Christianity, with its semi-pessimism and its gospel of indiscriminate, short-sighted pity has but thwarted Nature, wiser and kinder by far, in her task of shaping the man into the More-than-man. As for Schopenhauer, he has but accentuated what is worst in Christianity and tried to find for it a philosophical basis."

It is plain that this More-than-man is somewhat of the "Gothic" and military type; that he is a spiritual descendant of the hordes of Northern barbarians who swept down on the effete Roman empire, and to whose fresh vigour, innocent alike of Greek ethics and of Christian saintliness, our European civilization largely owes its birth and progress. Needless to say that this Superman might be more properly called the Superbrute; that he competes on just the same plane of merely psychic selfish existence as other animals, although through the development of his reason he has left all competitors behind.

This ideal has been easily and freely criticized. It is easy to show that the self-giving as well as the self-seeking instincts are essential to the survival of species; that brutal unmitigated egotism is a principle of decadence and deterioration; that competition obtains only in regard to material goods of limited divisible quantity, and to the conditions of merely animal life; that violence is not strength; that society is the condition of individuality; that the social instinct is the complement of the individual instinct; and so forth.

But it is far more important to recognize the confused gropings after a better conception of perfect manhood; the revolt against an exaggerated pessimism which excludes all possibility of God's Will being done on earth as it is in heaven; the revolt against a transcendental mysticism that finds the theatre of man's highest life only in the clouds; against a sentimental, enervating pity that views pain and sorrow as the sovereign unmitigated evils, and fosters a blind self-defeating "indiscriminate charity"; against the confusion of gentleness with softness, of meekness with weakness; against an overstraining of the "organic" idea of Society and against kindred theories of government and authority, socialistic or absolutist, which are fatal to the growth of personality and to the truly Christian principle of individual dignity. We should sympathize with the scorn of contented mediocrity, of the average and paltry; with the feeling that in some sense a man should "be himself" and not the creature of servile imitation and conformity; with the aspiration after the "strong man," the hero, the More-than-man, whose production is the goal of all moral endeavour. For all his monstrosity, the Superman is largely built up of, and lives by, certain too neglected elements of the Christian ideal of perfect manhood. He represents a revolt, although an excessive and indiscriminate revolt, against false mysticism and false sentiment. He moves at once away from and nearer to Christ in the same circle or orbit. The ideal is not all of iron or earth, and whatever admixture of heavenly gold it may possess we have a right to seek the same, pure and unalloyed, in the ideal manhood of Christ.

XIII
THE SUPERMAN, FALSE AND TRUE

That by which man is man, is the spirit; distinctively human life is spirit-life. Man is a spirit; and to make God intelligible to man, in the highest terms known to man, revelation tells us "God is a spirit." Man's best life is a divine life, an imitation of God's life so far as we can realize or comprehend it: "Be ye therefore perfect, as your Father in heaven is perfect." As before, we leave aside the metaphysical problem of the relation of the Divine Being to our own, of sameness and otherness, and speak simply of those manifestations of the spirit of which man's soul is the theatre, though God is also their author in some mysterious way.

There is another life in man which is not spiritual, but psychic, or even animal; subservient to the higher; a lower stage through which he has to pass: to which he ever relapses when he ceases to struggle upward. Of this life the Superman is the highest and most heroic development. Let us remember that it is not nothing because it is not all; that it does not—because it is evil as an end—cease to be good and useful as a means, a divinely ordained means. Manichean exaggerations that have crept into our piety and falsified our asceticism, "forbidding to marry and commanding to abstain from meats," are partly answerable for the appearance of the Superman. The Gospel forbids sovereign solicitude, not moderated care, for the psychic life. The self-regarding instincts are its governing motive power. In its absolute purity it exists nowhere in man. Even in the worst of us the Spirit intervenes at times and subordinates the lower life to the higher, sacrificing, or wishing to sacrifice, the interests of the separate Self to those of objective Truth and Right, to the interests of God and of the Spirit. There is "honour among thieves"; nor is the disinterested sense of Justice for others ever wholly extinguished. Rightly interpreted, this is a sense of union with God, a sense that the universal interests of the Divine Will are also our own deepest and truest interests, to which our separate interests should give way. This is Conscience, and Conscience sleeps, but never dies; it is a "worm that dieth not and a fire that is not quenched."

To the vigour of the psychic life of self-love we owe large results of human development, individual and social,—results that in many ways stimulate and prophetically foreshadow those of the spirit-life. It has developed a desire for truth as an instrument of life; for that knowledge which is power; an esteem of right and justice as conditions of social progress; an esteem of fine arts as a means of subjective enjoyment. It is the struggle for existence, for enjoyment, for personal advantages of all kinds that has made man work hard and has sharpened his wits and has taught him the useful arts and has discovered for him the secrets of nature; it is a provident self-interest that has taught him the value of association with others and that he must give and serve if he would get and be served. In societies where commerce and competition are rampant and spiritual influences largely discredited, we can see very fairly what wonderful, if not very admirable, results are produced by the psychic life. Such societies tend to realize the Gospel idea of a "Kingdom of this World," a " Kingdom of Satan," whose children are wiser in their generation than the children of light—naturally enough ; for the lower and older forms of life are deeper-rooted than the newer and higher.

Yet for all its possible abuses, the psychic life is for man the condition of the spiritual; he needs the meat that perisheth as well as the meat that endureth. It is the quest for the former that has raised him to a level in which his need of the latter has made itself definitely felt. The blind instinct of self-love, of regard for this separate organism destined to be the theatre or instrument of the spirit-life, is therefore from God ; a rule and guide, but not a sovereign rule ; good as a servant, bad as a master.

However indefinitely the psychic life may be developed above the level of animalism or savagery through man's superior mentality and power of self-control which can be pressed into the service of egoism, yet its fundamental character remains unchanged ; it is the life of one atom among an infinite multitude, of one moment in limitless time ; of a mere point that would make itself the universe, relating all to itself ; and yet whose insignificance is simply immeasurable.

It is with Conscience in the widest acceptation—

moral, intellectual, and æsthetic Conscience—that the spirit-life begins; with the sense of universal, imperative interests to which those of one's separate self must be wholly subordinate, interests which are identically the same for every spiritual being; with the sense that we are, or ought to be, before all else, instruments of the Divine Will, manifestations of the Divine Life, finding thereby our true, abiding, immeasurable significance and dignity. Of this "over-individual" life of disinterested devotion to divine ends it is said: "I live, yet not I [the separate Self], but Christ [the spiritual Self] liveth in Me," or again: "I in them and Thou in Me." Yet if it is a divine life it is also that life by which man is man; or, if we choose to call the psychic life "human" and "natural" in an unfavourable sense, the spirit-life is the life by which man becomes "Superman" and puts on the likeness of God. It is, moreover, a supernatural life to which the psychic or "natural" man cannot attain by his own methods or motives. All he can do is to learn his own limits, the futility of his ends and desires, to dash himself despairingly against the barriers that shut him in. He can rise to the sense of a Beyond and the need of a Beyond; but to believe in it, to live for it firmly and prevalently, he cannot. This is something which must be given to him; for which he is as dependent on Providence as he is for the bread that perisheth; for the rain and the sunshine and other conditions without which all his husbandry were in vain.

And if our science is so slow to understand, to arrange, classify, and connect, the fragments of that world which is given to our outer senses, and to which our organic, psychic self belongs, is it wonderful that our understanding should be infinitely slower to piece together those experiences that are given it from within; especially, since the nature of language requires that they should be expressed in terms and symbols drawn from the world of sense? Is it wonderful that the spirit-life should be so essentially mysterious and full of seeming contradictions, and that to determine the relations of the spirit to God should be as difficult as to define the spirit or to define God? If then the true Superman is necessarily the spiritual man, it is vain to look for him in any development however vigorous of the psychic life. His type is not to be sought in the first or psychic Adam, "of the earth earthy," but in the second Adam, who is "the Lord from Heaven."

XIV
RÉSUMÉ

True devotion to Christ means believing in Him, heart and soul, as the true life, the divine type of manhood; it means sameness of spirit, identity of interest, unity of aim, conformity of action; it means the only kind of sympathy and discipleship which He supremely desires and values: "Weep not for Me, but weep for yourselves and your children"— that is, Weep not *for* Me; but *with* Me; weep for that divine cause for which I live and die; for Me, only as for the embodiment of that cause. To reproduce His spirit in us is the sole end, justification, and criterion of the Catholic Church and all her institutions and teachings—to make us More-than-men, Sons of God;—an elementary truth, but, just for that reason, easily obscured and confused.

Looking then to the archetype of perfect manhood as portrayed in the Gospels we find a spirit free from every blemish of "Sentimentality," "Mysticality," or "Practicality," yet, in its simplicity, embracing and overpassing the excellences which these exaggerate and violently tear asunder.

Certainly, the first and most obvious impression is that of a loving personality, full of sweetness, tenderness, and compassion, entering readily into all the joys and sorrows of those around. As contrasted with the austerity and asceticism of the Baptist, He presents Himself as one who comes eating and drinking, the friend of publicans and sinners, a Bridegroom whose presence diffuses joy on all sides, and forbids fasting and mourning. He is one who delights to be with the children of men, rather than alone in the desert; one who embraces little children and is at home with the birds of the air and the lilies of the field, who wanders happy and improvident among the hedgerows and the cornfields; one who sees a Heavenly Father's love in the rain and the sunshine and in all that happens; one who squanders compassion and forgiveness on all around, merciless only to the merciless; to all others merciful and indulgent on the sole condition that they too shall be merciful and indulgent.

This plainly is the temper of one whose own heart overflows with love and tenderness. With such, feeling is apt to assume the reins of spiritual government to the prejudice of insight and action. The subjective satisfaction becomes an end in itself; the appetite for the luxury of emotion grows strong and tyrannical by indulgence. Feelings, we have already shown, are false or true according to the implicit judgments which they embody. When they are thus fostered for their own sake, they necessarily become false and lose touch with reality. They need to be continually clarified by intelligence, solidified by action. Those to whom a sentimental Christ is congenial dwell too exclusively on the lineaments just indicated. For the rest they find the Gospels "dry" and needing to be supplemented by pious imagination. Their Christ and, by consequence, their God, is apt to become wholly emasculate, void of all ethical vigour, of all mystical depth, the apotheosis of universal amiability and indiscriminate indulgence. The religion which worships such an ideal is of necessity decadent and feeble; and is characterized by a whittling away of the substance of the moral law, and by a stagnation of all intelligent interest in the mysteries of God.

But if we look more closely at the Gospel portrait, we soon realize the utter superficiality of the sentimentalist's impression. We find that the Love there presented to us is the fruit of deep vision; that it is fed from the very foundations of truth to which its roots reach down; that if Christ is tender it is because He is true; that if He is merciful it is because He is just and because so often the gentler judgment is the more just, the harsher judgment the more narrow and irrational. We find that He can also be severe and unyielding, just because His love is long-sighted, a strength and not a weakness. Moreover, it is a love that does not rest in and feed on itself; it is an energy, an enthusiasm that embodies itself in will and action ; in labour and suffering on behalf of Righteousness and Truth, on behalf of the Kingdom of God in the soul of man.

To other eyes the Gospel presents the figure mainly of a mystic and ascetic. They find one to whom this world was little more than an idle dream on the point of vanishing for ever in the already breaking dawn of eternity; one who lived solely in and for the mysterious Beyond; whose message was: "Repent, for the Kingdom of Heaven is at hand"; one whose doctrine of self-denial and renunciation was largely based on a sense of the speedy evanescence of all temporal and earthly values. Still more does He come before them in the writings of St. John and St. Paul as one impregnated with the sense of eternal realities, for whom the fleshly veil has grown transparent; who descends to earth by an effort, but rises naturally to heaven; who lives in the presence and by the light of Divinity; ever absorbingly conscious of Himself as the Word of God.

And from this they are apt to pass to a conception of a purely contemplative and ascetical Christ, who finds the whole substance and essence of the spirit-life in the exercise of intellectual vision to which feeling and action are but subordinate conditions or concomitants. In this they rend at once the unity of Christ and the unity of the spirit-life. They soon begin to shelter under Gospel authority a mysticism and asceticism far more pagan than Christian,—a mysticism which sets the supernatural at discord with the natural, which looks for the divine as breaking into, rather than blending with, the human; which seeks God not through and behind the realm of Law and Order, but in supposed oases of interspersed chaos; and an asceticism grounded on a false trust in those visions and experiences of abnormal mentality to which the "corpus sanum" is an impediment and which are favoured by nervous exhaustion and derangement; the asceticism not only of Gnostics, but of dervishes and fakirs and of all who implicitly hold that body and spirit are essentially antagonistic and derived from antagonistic principles. The Johannine and Pauline antithesis of flesh and spirit, together with the example of Him who was "poor and in labours from His youth up," who had not where to lay His head, who fasted in the desert, and spent long nights in prayer, whose sufferings and death were in a certain sense self-inflicted and voluntary, all may easily be, and have often been, invoked to favour such a view.

But here again closer inspection reveals the superficialty and onesidedness of this presentment of Perfect Manhood. If Christ is not Love alone, neither is He Light alone. To sever these interests of Feeling and Vision, to make either principal, is as impossible as to sever the warmth and the brilliancy of sunshine. Still less possible is it to find in Christ that hostility to feeling and affection, that frigid detachment from all mortal ties and necessities, that abstract aloofness from the world of sinful, suffering humanity, which are the almost indispensable conditions of a life devoted entirely to intellectual contemplation, to an effort to realize permanently the condition of angels while still in the flesh.

True it is that the perfect simultaneous exercise and balance of the lives of feeling, thought, and action are not possible; that it is by the alternating emphasis now of one, now of another, that a harmony of successive parts is to be secured. Hence the life of sentiment or of activity that is not interrupted by explicit contemplative effort with more or less frequency becomes quickly impoverished and earthly. Yet equally true it is that the contemplative effort cannot be permanently maintained without predudice to mind and body and to the whole life of the spirit; but needs to be steadied and rested by action, and brought into contact with feeling and reality. Else there results a complete upset of the psycho-physiological balance, whose fruits are illusions and hallucinations on the part of injured mind, while the body, left masterless, avenges by its rebellion the wrongs done to it by a morbid asceticism. "How often have I seen those who were fed with the bread of angels delighting in the husks of swine!" says à Kempis. Such a fall may conceivably be a Divine punishment of spiritual pride; but more often it is the result of misguidance, ignorance, or well-meaning indiscretion. It is the vengeance of Nature on those who ignore or defy her laws, which are indeed, after all, the Will of God. We may then be confident that the spirit-life as revealed to us in Christ is not, in any morbid sense of the terms, mystical or ascetical.

To the far greater number of average common-sense people who pride themselves on a freedom from sentiment and mysticism, the eminently practical side of Christ's spirit will make a strong appeal. His vehement insistence on good works as the fruit and criterion of faith ; His repudiation of the devotion which says "Lord, Lord," and stops there, of the affection based on natural relations of kinship, friendship, and nationality, and not on unity of aim and work; His life of vigorous, active, self-sacrificing devotion to His Father's business,—to teaching, healing, saving, ministering; His conflict unto death with the powers of evil ; and then, His opposition to theorists and doctrinaires, to those who preached salvation by dialectic and would make religion primarily intellectual and speculative; His disdain of prophecy and miracle and of any other preternatural criterion of discipleship as compared with the criterion of that charity of experimental goodness that feeds the hungry and clothes the naked,—all this and much more, makes out an easy and most plausible case for "Practicality." *Circuibat benefaciendo:* He went about doing good. "Doing good" seems to be the whole of the matter ; more especially that sort of good that involves "going about." Conduct, in this narrow, practical sense, is indeed, as Matthew Arnold says, three-quarters of life for the vast majority of mankind. Naturally then the importance of the Gospel seems to lie wholly in its bearing on this sort of conduct. Hence the tendency to regard philanthropic activity as the substance of Christianity; to absorb oneself in works of parochial, social, national, and international beneficence; to merge one's whole personality in the organism of the community; to forget that when all are sufficiently fed, clothed, housed, and tended, the question still remains: What to do with life,—a question which they cannot answer to whom philanthropy is the whole of life.

Philanthropy is Christian so far as it means a denial of self for the sake of others, a subordination of the particular to the general interest. But it easily consists with a somewhat materialized view of the general or universal good and describes it as "the greatest happiness of the greatest number." This means estimating action by its external fruitfulness rather than by its subjective and spiritual quality. Under the influence of this view conscientious people often scruple to follow the less extensively and quantitatively beneficent course, and will perhaps neglect themselves or their own homes in order to minister in city slums. The "Universal Good" to which self must give way is simply the ethical "Ought." It is that which is good and right absolutely, and not in reference to myself or to others. Altruism no less than Egoism has to bow before this sovereign rule. They are few who have the power or opportunity of working for the many. But they are still fewer, if there be any, who have not both power and opportunity of self-forgetful devotion, of actions which, externally insignificant, are, on their spiritual and subjective side, of eternal and absolutely universal importance.

If Christ's spirit was practical, it was certainly not

utilitarian. If it disdained faith without works, it also disdained works without faith. We see that in Him the inward and the outward were organically connected; that they were but different aspects of one and the same spiritual life and action, a life that was at once Vision and Love and Will; that His love was active and His action loving, and that both were penetrated by the light of truth. Now one, and now another aspect of that spirit-life would be emphasized or brought into play, according to the exigencies of the moment; but at the centre they were all merged in, and sprang from, that which is at once all of them and none of them, which is simply Spirit and Life. Drawn forth momentarily from that centre, each of them—Love, Vision, Will—was still quickened at its root by an infusion of the other two; and returning to the centre again, invigorated by exercise, became to them in turn a source of enriched vitality.

All idea of priority or principality or of true separableness among these elements of the spirit-life must be abandoned, if we are to read the Gospels aright and to grasp the conception of Perfect Manhood there presented to us. If we would arrive at such a conception we cannot do better than try to apprehend the spirit of Christ just as it breathes itself forth in that prayer whose words He has adopted, but whose sense and inspiration (of which they are the vehicle) are all His own, and can only be determined in the light of all His teaching and action.

This prayer of Christ is at once the deepest and

most succinct expression of the Spirit and Life of Christ, of that Life whose reproduction in ourselves is the criterion of our religious beliefs and institutions. It is the norm of all pure prayer and indirectly of all pure belief; it is at once the *Lex Orandi* and the *Lex Credendi*. The *Credo* is but the "explicitation" of what is latent in the *Pater noster*.

PART II

THE PRAYER OF CHRIST

I
THE PERFECT PRAYER

SURELY it must have seemed like a momentary descent of the spirit of peace on the angry tumult of primeval chaos when, in the name of the oldest and widest Christian Communion (and doubtless by a prophetic instinct of that same spirit), a Roman Cardinal, in the year 1893, opened the Chicago Parliament of Religions with the simple prayer taught by Jesus to the fishermen of Galilee nearly two thousand years before.

At its height the wave pauses before it dashes itself in foam and confusion upon the shore. Such a brief instant of pause, of inward silence, must have been felt in that spiritual Babel ere the many tongues were let loose in the interest of their multitudinous creeds and contentions. It was as when the little child in their midst stood as a mute rebuke to the worse than childish contentions of the chosen Twelve. It was a recall to simplicity, to directness, to the one thing needful; to the point whence all had diverged and scattered, as sheep issuing from the pen, and to which all must converge again, as sheep gathered into the fold at evening. And surely from any other lips than those of a prince of the court of Rome the prayer had lacked the same fulness of significance.

A man's spirit utters itself to some degree in every voluntary movement of his life; but never so fully and perfectly as in prayer—prayer that is really his own. For prayer is "the lifting up of the heart and mind to God"; it is an act in which vision, feeling, and will, the three factors of the spirit-life, designedly blend together and strive to attain their highest and deepest expression. In prayer the spirit pierces down to the root and beginning of all reality from which it springs, and stretches up to the end and summit of all reality towards which it strains and struggles; and between these two poles lies the whole sphere of the finite which it strives to compass and transcend. In prayer it expressly deals with the Ultimates; with the first and the last and, in reference to them, with all that lies between them. And in this contact with Reality it attains Truth—truth of vision, truth of feeling, truth of will.

There is a sense in which the whole spirit-life may be called prayer; for it is, indeed, communion with God. *Laborare est orare*—to work is to pray, to think is to pray, to love is to pray. But we do not now speak merely of this implicit and practical prayer; but of conscious explicit prayer, in which the spirit is concentrated expressly on the religious aspect of life—on God, or on things precisely in their relation to God. We speak, not of the prayer which is "lived," but of the prayer which is "prayed."

In such prayer the spirit-life finds its fullest embodiment. Here we find what a man *is* in his deepest self—if only the prayer be real, his very own. Yet even in those prayers that are most deeply our own, prayers of the spirit at its highest tension, the words and conceptions in which they normally embody themselves are never wholly our own; they belong to the language and tradition which we inherit. They are our own only in so far as they are inspired by the inward prayer; in so far, namely, as the spirit, like the whirlwind that sweeps up the autumn leaves in its vortex, rearranging and ordering them after the pattern of its own movement, seizes instinctively from the mind's treasury the words and images most congenial to its need of self-expression and weaves them into a living garment, in which its own form and movements become visible.

Taken singly and literally, the several phrases of the Lord's Prayer were familiar to every pious Jew of that day. They were then, and they are now, to be found up and down in the Old Testament, in the sacred books and liturgy of the Hebrew people. So far, they were our Lord's only by tradition and by adoption. Studied literally, without respect to His whole life and personality, and simply by an analysis of the words and expressions as they were then valued by any ordinary Jew, they could never yield us a distinctively Christian sense. We must, therefore, try to seize them as they fell from His lips, still aglow with His spirit; we must take them not one by one, each complete in itself, but as part of a complex, organic whole, each in the light of all the rest, and all in the light of His whole life of action and utterance;

we must look to the sayer as well as to what is said. Else our study will be of the dead letter, the skeleton, the empty husk of that prayer. For a prayer is a vital utterance, or it is nothing; no dissection of the lifeless corpse can discover the soul.

Yet, on the other hand, it must be remembered that the "Our Father" is not given to us as a prayer which our Lord Himself prayed, but as one which He taught His disciples to pray. Though this fact does not make it any less truly an expression of his own spirit, with which they too were to be filled, yet it allows us to attach more significance to the actual form of words than we should be otherwise quite justified in doing. For the words in which vehement desire escapes from the heart straight into the ears of God (the Reader of Hearts, to whom even our unworded desires are eloquent), are not calculated with a view to reveal that desire to our fellow-men. According as the prayer is more real and vehement, its utterance tends to be more broken, interjectory, with strong cries like those of Gethsemani and Golgotha; less reasoned, less connected, less discursive; at times tumultuous and incoherent, as the impatient spirit hopelessly tumbles over and ransacks its vocabulary in search of words for its unutterable need; while in moments of utmost tension speech may be completely paralysed.

But the words of the "Our Father" were intended to convey to the disciples our Lord's spirit of prayer; they were addressed to their human understanding and not to the Divine Omniscience. As such, they possess a certain degree of that reasoned completeness and unity which belong to an instruction. We must remember, therefore, that they are accommodated to the intelligence, to the customary modes of religious thought and speech, familiar to the simple folk of Galilee; that they belong far more to the language of prophecy than to that of philosophy. The expression which they give to our Lord's own inward prayer and spirit is, no doubt, the best and highest possible within such limits of thought and speech; but that it is infinitely inadequate cannot be denied, and should not be forgotten. The Master-Artist works here with the rude materials to hand; and to some extent their very rudeness reveals His mastery. His whole spirit is here, as it is even in the least of its manifestations; but not so wholly or clearly manifested as it might have been in a higher medium of expression, or in the language of angels.

Language, like outward sensation, is at best suggestive—a few points, a few lines which the responsive mind fills in from the storehouse of memory, and so more than half creates the object of its apprehension. According, therefore, to the extent and kind of our own spiritual experiences shall we be able to seize some measure of the spirit, at best rudely hinted in the words of the Lord's Prayer. "My sheep hear My voice"; only because the spirit of Christ is already in us can it be strengthened, educated, and developed from without through the instrumentality of words. Without such inward responsiveness no clarity or perfection of outward expression would avail; but when spiritual sympathy quickens the inward ear the obscurest whisper is a revelation of spirit to spirit.

It will help much, therefore, in all cases first to determine as exactly as we can just what sense our Lord's words must have conveyed to His hearers' minds, independently of the heart response which they elicited from those whose spirit was closer to His own; to determine, that is, the current value of those words for the religious thought and language of Galilee two thousand years ago. This is no easy task. For centuries the Church has pondered this prayer in her heart, and has loaded every phrase with a growing wealth of meaning, according as she has penetrated more deeply into the implications of Christ's spirit. Thus, much that was latent and confused for former times has become for us clear and explicit; and it needs some effort of well-instructed historic imagination to put ourselves back to the beginning of this process of expansion, to realize what "fatherhood" and "heaven" and "the kingdom" and "daily bread" and "temptation" and the "evil one" meant, and were intended to mean, for Peter and Andrew and the sons of Zebedee.

For this meaning must in some way be the criterion of any fuller sense our own minds may then attach to these same terms; of any attempt to find a re-embodiment for the same prayer-spirit in our own language and modes of thought and to pour, without spilling a drop, the contents of the old vessel into the new. For the spirit abides unchanged through all changes of thought and speech; man's mind transforms itself ceaselessly, but in the depths of his heart, where God meets him, he is always the same. Could Christ teach us, His disciples of to-day, to pray, the language would be different, for it would be our own; but the spirit and substance would be the same. As it is, we must seek that spirit through the language and thoughts of the Galilean fishermen of two thousand years ago.

II
DEFECTIVE TYPES

St. Luke (xi. 1-4) gives the Lord's Prayer in an abbreviated, St. Matthew (vi. 9-15) in an amplified, form. We may be sure that neither the omissions in one case, nor the expansions in the other, are substantial, although it is the amplified form which has obtained permanent footing in the Church. St. Matthew introduces the prayer into the Sermon on the Mount as illustrating, by way of contrast, our Lord's admonition against certain false conceptions of prayer, Jewish and Pagan. St. Luke represents it as given by our Lord, on another occasion, in answer to the request of one of His disciples: "Lord, teach us to pray, as John also taught his disciples." Thus, in both cases, it is presented to us explicitly as a norm or ideal of what prayer ought to be. It is opposed both to two false standards and to a less perfect standard.

It is (1) the prayer of those who seek the glory of God and not the glory of men; it is (2) the prayer of those who would raise man to the likeness of God, not of those who would lower God to the likeness of man.

It is (3) the prayer of the children of the bride-chamber, of those who have at least crossed the threshold of the kingdom; not of those who still strain towards its borders, and for whom it is yet an ideal, not a reality.

I

Two types of prayer are signalled out for us altogether repugnant to the spirit of Christ.

Of these, by far the more reprehensible is the prayer of the hypocrite or actor, whose offence does not consist in the fact that he prays in public, but that he does so for the sake of publicity and in order that he may be seen and praised of men. Our Lord Himself had been praying in public, or at least before others, when the disciple said to Him: "Lord, teach us to pray." And He even bids us let our light shine before men, " that they may see our good works"; but then it is to be in such a way that they may glorify, not us, but our Father who is in heaven. Plainly He would have us look directly and immediately to the inside of the cup and platter and leave the outside to look after itself, confident that if the heart be right all will be right. A deliberate aiming at edification and outward righteousness, like a deliberate aiming at happiness, defeats itself; it becomes self-conscious, self-complacent, hypocritical. If the true light is in us, it will shine through us unawares and bring glory to God. To feed the flame in our hearts is our concern; the shining is God's; we are not even to think about it: "Let not thy left hand know what thy right hand doeth."

It is as food for self-complacency that the hypocrite

desires the approbation of others, that he may contemplate a flattering image of himself mirrored in a multitude of minds. What our Lord would exclude is, at root, spiritual self-complacency. Secrecy from others is important only as a means to secrecy from oneself. Here, as everywhere else, the outward is valued merely for the sake of the inward. A man may enter into his oratory and shut the door and pray—yet not in secret. He may be no less of an actor than if he stood at the street-corner or in the synagogue. On the other hand, the Pharisee and the publican both prayed openly in the temple, yet the latter is as plainly a type of secrecy in prayer as the former is of hypocrisy or acting. What, then, is the inward spiritual secrecy symbolized by the outward, but by no means to be identified with it?

It is the disposition of the soul which realizes that in prayer it stands before a "Father who sees in secret"; One to whom all hearts are open, all desires known, from whom no secret is hid; One, therefore, before whom it is utterly vain to pose, to act, to pretend to be other than we really are. To some extent we must think of God and deal with Him humanwise, as we deal with our fellow-men, with our parents, our rulers, before whom we are always tempted to act a part, to seem better than we are. But, so far as prayer is a "raising of the heart and mind to God," it is a deliberate effort to rise above this limit of our imagination on the wings of faith, to put ourselves honestly face to face with conscience, with the Father who seeth in secret. This is what the publican did, though he prayed openly in the temple, and what the

Pharisee could not have done had he even entered into his chamber and shut the door. And why not? For surely the educated Pharisee was far more capable than the theologically untrained publican of a more spiritual view of God's nature.

If such elevation of view depended on philosophical training it would go hard with the world at large. But in truth it depends only on a disposition of the heart. It is not the intellectual man, but the spiritual man, who apprehends God spiritually. For the intellectual man may be morally on the psychic level still, self-centered, worldly, and even animal. If so, his God will necessarily be in his own image and likeness; One with whom he will deal as individual with individual, as self with self; One with whom he can make a bargain, an adjustment of mutual interests; not One whose interests are realized as indistinguishable from his own.

But in moments when a man rises, however briefly, to the spiritual level, and yields himself to the imperative, unconditional claims of conscience, of truth, of principle; when he loses his separate self, with its separate interests, in the consciousness of being before all else the servant and instrument of a divine and universal Will—in such moments he can view himself only from the standpoint of that divine "over-individual" interest, and as he really is; all motives for self-flattery melt away as illusions and dreams; he can but see himself with the eyes of his Father, who seeth in secret; he can but strike his breast and cry: "God, be merciful to me a sinner." Here there is an entire absorption in God's point of view, in God's will and interest; a complete dying to one's own, so far as separate from God's or separable. It is as when for a brief space we forget ourselves absolutely in the sorrows or desires of another, and lend our whole being to the service of that other, with whom we are made one just for the moment. Such moments of union with God's view and feeling and will are graces given to all from time to time; to multiply them till they become fused and continuous is the whole aim of mystic endeavour.

Prayer, therefore, like fasting or almsgiving, if it is not to be a mere doing or saying, must be an action of the spirit-life, not of the psychic life; it must be the utterance of vision and feeling, proceeding from the spirit and the heart, from the secret chamber where the soul meets God as the stem meets its root in the bosom of the earth.

As little would our Lord condemn public prayer as He would condemn public almsgiving, or fasting, or other overt good works. He would but teach us that the intention of the hypocrite or actor in seeking publicity simply excludes that self-forgetfulness through which alone the soul can meet God as a spirit on the spiritual plane. On that plane all self-consciousness of the lower sort (that is, all consciousness of the narrow, individual self, whose interests can be conceived as other than God's) vanishes for the time being; all inward "acting" is laid aside, because the desires and motives that would prompt it are annihilated. The same perfect simplicity, directness, and sincerity are attained in such prayer as in the unself-conscious beneficence which asks in wonder: "Lord, when saw we Thee hungry and fed Thee?"

2

If some sort of visible and external religious society is undoubtedly necessary for the waking and education of our spiritual life—since consistent individualism in religion is as sterilizing as in other spiritual interests, such as science and general culture—it follows that public prayer and worship are as necessary in their place as secret prayer; that they foster secret prayer in the same way that public intelligence and taste foster private intelligence and taste.

But public prayer must necessarily be couched in words and symbols in which the common spirit finds common utterance. As little as Christ would condemn public prayer in condemning the hypocrites, so little would He reject vocal prayer or forms of prayer when He warns us against much speaking and vain repetitions. Galilee of the Gentiles may easily have familiarized His Jewish hearers with the heathen practices here denounced; and that materialism of thought, which materialism of life so invariably introduces into every religion, rendered His warnings by no means superfluous for a people who were at all times only too readily infected by surrounding idolatry and superstition. More particularly did this point of Christ's teaching need to be recorded and emphasized for the benefit of those Gentile Christians who had crowded into the Church by the time that St. Matthew's Gospel was written, and whom the laws of mental inertia and "least resistance" disposed to retain as much of their old religious tradition as could possibly receive any sort of Christian interpretation. What with their own inevitable tendency to receive Judaic-Christian traditions in a Gentile sense, and with the Church's wise willingness to tolerate, baptize, and reinterpret, rather than destroy, all those ideas and symbols of paganism that might serve as a more flexible vessel for the new wine of the Gospel than Judaism would offer, there must have been a continual danger for the early Gentile Christians lest the older and deeper habit of mind should rise up again and vanquish the new.

We have only to acquaint ourselves with some of the lower phases of contemporary religion to realize what is meant by this "battalogy," this babbling or gabbling or vain repetition which our Lord reprehends. It is the prayer of those who think that they will be heard for their "much speaking," and that quantity of prayer is as important or more important than quality; who attach a certain *ex opere operato* value to bare words, apart from the inward prayer which they should embody; who hope to weary their gods into compliance with their own will. An error so ancient, enduring, and universally recurrent is sure to be "natural" in some sense, and to have some plausible justification.

When we would move the tardy and reluctant will of our fellow-man we know—and every beggar and every spoilt child knows—that insistence and reiteration count for much; that each request makes some little impression, were it only as a drop of water on a stone, and that the accumulation of such impressions may at last break down the most stubborn opposition. Has not Christ Himself told us the story of the importunate widow, just to teach us that we should always pray and never weary? As long as men conceive their God humanwise—not as a spirit, not as a Father who sees in secret—it is but natural that they should treat with Him as with a man; that they should think it necessary to acquaint Him with their inward desires; that they should hope to weary Him with repetitions, to cajole and flatter Him with praises; and that they should attach more importance and effectuality to their words than to their desires. Hence the ceaseless tongue-clatter distinctive of pagan worship, the hurrying through of formulas, the measuring of prayers by their number, length, time, etc.

If true prayer is a raising of man's heart and mind to God, it can be no true prayer which simply lowers God to the heart and mind of man. To some extent such a lowering is inevitable while man is on earth and God in heaven. He must stoop, and stoop almost infinitely, to meet us; but if there be no straining upwards on our part, no effort to raise our thoughts and desires to a diviner and more spiritual level, the essence of prayer is absent. Not only does the mechanical lip-service drag God down to the level of man's mind, but also to the level of his heart. It is importunate in a bad sense; it endeavours to force and weary the divine will into conformity with man's unpurified will; to wring from it a reluctant consent to man's natural psychic desires. Only while we think of God humanwise is it possible to imagine that our desires should be better and wiser than His; or that He should yield to that which He knows to be less good and wise. But when we remember that no prayer avails but that which the Holy Spirit puts into our heart, and which is therefore an expression of the Divine Will; that we are told to seek first the Kingdom of God and His righteousness, and all else only in reference to that end—then it is manifest that the importunate prayer which Christ commends is that which struggles to bring man's will into conformity with God's, not God's into conformity with man's; that which raises man's heart up to God, not that which drags God down to man's heart.

Yet to sweep aside as so much rubbish and superstition all the rosaries and litanies, Christian and non-Christian, that have busied man's lips since he first began lisping his prayers to God, would be as foolish as to condemn all public prayer on the score of hypocrisy. Formality is the evil, not form, nor even formulas. Is not the "Our Father" a divinely sanctioned form or formula? Prayer, like every movement of the spirit, necessarily tends to embody itself, to become explicit in words and symbols. And this embodiment is an aid to its development, just as our whole spiritual life is shaped and fostered by our religious beliefs, and shapes them, in return, by a process of action and reaction involved in the unity of our faculties of thought, feeling, and will. As proceeding from the most hidden depths of the spirit, where it finds its roots in God, prayer does not lend itself readily to formulation, and the attempt to give it exact verbal expression must be largely unsuccessful unless it be a prayer of the mind's surface, rather than of the heart's centre. Hence there is much more unreality and formalism in a discursive, well-reasoned address to Heaven than in the broken aspirations and reiterated cries forced from the soul by the pressure of its travail. The confessed irrelevance between the words used and the intention behind them, which would be preposterous in the dealings of man with man, may in prayer give the heart a freedom of movement which an endeavour at exactitude of expression would destroy; while it implies, or may imply, a recognition that the prayer is addressed to One who sees in secret, who considers our desires rather than our halting words. Thus there is no condemnation passed on forms and repetitions, but only on formality and on vain repetitions, on the merely quantitative and mechanical view of prayer. We should not then admit it as a reproach when attention is drawn to the likeness between many points of Catholic and ethnic worship, as in this matter of rosaries and litanies, forms and repetitions. We see in it a proof that such practices are the spontaneous natural creation of man's religious needs—needs which the Church purifies and to which she ministers. Nor will the disciples of Him who so often held up the heathen and the Samaritan to our imitation allow for a moment that all the formulas and repetitions of heathenism are vain; or that in them the true spirit of prayer never finds blind utterance; or that the cries which blameless ignorance sends up to false gods never enter into the ears of the true.

H

Like faith, superstition is an affair of the heart far more than of the mind. Where the object or motive of prayer is non-moral, psychic, selfish, no orthodoxy of mental conception or verbal expression will save such prayer from superstition. On the other hand, if the motive be spiritual, ethical, inspired by the love of goodness and not by the love of self, no theological error or crudeness of form will affect the substantial purity of such a prayer. Of its own nature, no doubt, the spirit tends to shape the mind into conformity with itself; materialism of life and affection tends to materialism of belief; purity of heart tends to spirituality of thought. But the process is tardy, and is worked out usually in the collective life of the religious community, rather than in the single life of the individual. The individual inherits the forms and conceptions of his people, and can modify them but slightly at best. His own spirit may be far too high or far too low for the medium of expression placed at his disposal by tradition; the prayer of the heathen to his idol may at times be less superstitious in spirit than that of the Christian to the true God.

3

" Lord, teach us to pray, as John also taught his disciples." Besides these two false standards of prayer —that of the hypocrite and that of the heathen— there is a true but less perfect standard to be contrasted with the Lord's Prayer, namely, the prayer of John the Baptist—greatest of those born of women, yet less than the least in the Kingdom of God.

The errors we have dealt with consist in bringing God down to the level of man's heart and mind in prayer, instead of raising man's heart and mind to God. They are begotten of man's great need to feel God close to him, like to him, and therefore manageable by him; to find in Him a powerful friend, or relation, or father, a "very present help in the time of trouble." Yet in the measure that we bring Him down to our level, we rob Him of the power of raising us up above ourselves. The more human He becomes, the less is He divine, all-seeing, all-mighty, all-loving, all-good. If He is our Father, it is because we have given Him our nature and likeness; it is because we have made Him man; not because He has made us more than men.

Contrary altogether to this debasing tendency was the spirit of the great prophets of Israel, of whom John the Baptist was chiefest, as nearest to Christ, as herald of the dawn. In them the sense of God's greatness, His otherness from man, His transcendence, was all-dominating, and filled them with a burning, reforming zeal against materialistic and unworthy conceptions of the divine majesty. Insistence on this truth brought home to men a sense of a measureless gulf interposed between God and themselves, of a distance and unlikeness hard to reconcile with the close relation of fatherhood. If the later prophets would at times turn abruptly from the preaching of God's awful might and majesty to the assurance of His fatherly love and compassion, yet it was rather with reference to Israel as a whole than to the individual sinner. For how could the individual dare to see in himself the filial counterpart of a being so transcendentally other and unlike himself? He listened, at best, in faith to promises of a coming Kingdom of Heaven in which men were to be transformed into sons of God, and were to sit at meat with God as children at their father's table. But that kingdom had not yet come. With the sense of God's greatness he had lost the sense of His nearness. He had yet to learn that the greatest is the lowliest, that the furthest is the nearest, that the most divine is the most human.

And this is a truth that revelation has made current coin among the least in the Kingdom of Heaven. It is the truth of which Christ was the living revelation; which became incarnate in Him who "gave to as many as received Him power to become the sons of God." Great and other as God was, yet men could become the sons of God, because they could become other and more than men; because the sense of nearness could be achieved otherwise than by materializing the spiritual, or by debasing God to man's image; it could be achieved by spiritualizing man and lifting him nearer to heaven. If then John the Baptist, like the other prophets, taught his followers some brief prayer embodying the spirit of his message and mission, it was but fitting that our Lord should do as much for the children of the bride-chamber; for they had lived to see what kings and prophets had vainly longed to see, namely, the Kingdom of God begun upon earth; and their hearts were filled with his own joy, with the fulness of that spirit which enabled them to cry: *Abba*, our Father.

III

THE INVOCATION

Pater noster qui es in cœlis.—Our Father who art in heaven

I

The invocation, "Our Father who art in heaven," is designed to bring the soul face to face with God in the secret chamber of the heart; to determine its attitude and disposition; to establish that due relation of mind, feeling, and will which is the condition of communion and converse between the creature and the Creator. When we call to another in our need, his name serves but to attract his attention; but when the child calls "Father," the appeal is not merely to the attention, but to the heart; it is a reminder of the relationship upon which the right to appeal is grounded.

The mother may for a moment forget the babe that clings to her breast; her attention may be diverted till a cry wins it back again. But the attention of the Heavenly Father is not diverted for a second; else we should return to nothingness: "He that keepeth Israel shall neither slumber nor sleep." It is not to call His attention to us, or to remind Him of claims which he never ceases to fulfil, but to recall our wandering soul to the consciousness of that love which, like the ether, ever surrounds and permeates us, that we need to cry out to Him.

2

In many of the ethnic religions the worship of departed ancestors has associated the notions of godhead and fatherhood. The title "Father" in such cases expresses principally the worshipper's sense of descent and derivation from the Deity. So also on the far higher plane of philosophical religions, where the term is applied in a quite metaphorical sense to the First Cause of all things, to the "deorum hominumque pater"—to "the Father of gods and men."

But in the ears of Peter, Andrew, and John the sense of the word "Father," as applied to God, was far more ethical than metaphysical. To a little child, untroubled about problems of Whence and Whither, the word "father" conveys no suggestion of descent or derivation. It stands for ethical relationships of love, care, protection, intimacy, authority. To the physical or metaphysical root of these relationships the child is indifferent. They themselves are matters of experience; their root is a matter of speculation—of inference from that experience. God's Fatherhood over Israel was a matter of history and experience for Christ's hearers. Israel was His well-beloved son, whom He had chosen and adopted; whom He had delivered from Egypt, fed and watched over in the desert, brought to the Land of Promise; whom He had borne with, chastened, and forgiven again and again with all the long-suffering and compassion of a Father. This, rather than any causal relationship, is what His Fatherhood meant for them. "I will be to him a Father, and he shall be to Me a son" implies a fatherhood and sonship of adoption rather than of nature. It was a mystery of God's free choice, a favour granted to Israel and denied to others: "Jacob have I loved, and Esau have I hated"; "He hath not done thus to any other nation, nor manifested His judgments to them." The fact that all alike were His creatures was not felt to be enough to make them all alike His children. The special and higher sense of sonship which belonged to Israel was interpreted exclusively as the only sense; if God loved Jacob, it seemed to follow that he must hate Esau. Depending on God's free choice rather than on His essential love, this Fatherhood over Israel was conditional on the obedience and reverence of the adopted son, whose sin or apostasy might break the bond. That it had not done so a thousand times, that God had forgiven again and again, was but another mystery of His inscrutable will.

With the growing sense of God's otherness and transcendent greatness, as revealed by the prophets, the distance of heaven from earth had been magnified in the general consciousness, while the sins of Israel rose ever higher as a barrier between them and the All-Holy, of whom righteousness was more and more clearly realized to be the central attribute. It was as when we wake to some unexpected greatness in a friend which seems to put him out of our reach and destroy all ease of intercourse. In us, though not in Him, some feeling of estrangement is inevitable; and He will need to give some new revelation of his unaltered affection, if he is to restore our confidence. So Christ came, as the newest and highest revelation of the Father's love, when Israel's sense of sonship had been weakened by the sense of God's transcendence and unlikeness, and of man's sinfulness. Who could dare to call Him Father whose infinitude seemed to exclude all possible likeness with the finite? Who could give men power to become the sons of so high and holy a God?

3

In one sense it is untrue, in another it is true, to say that Christ first revealed to men the Fatherhood of God. What was an occasional flash of intuition for the greater prophets, was with Him an abiding vision of which His whole life was one continuous utterance. The relative purity and tranquillity of heart, which at times allowed them a glimpse of the sources or roots of the spirit-life, was in His case absolute and constant. He looked down through the depths of His own spirit as through a crystal well of light into the abyss of all life and being, into the bosom of God, "the Father of spirits." "No man," no prophet, not even the greatest born of woman, "hath seen God at any time; the only begotten who is in the bosom of the Father, He hath declared Him."

In this vision He beheld the root and reason of that fatherliness of affection and care, which to Israel had seemed but a mystery of God's inscrutable will. He saw that in all its degrees, from the least to the greatest, it was founded on true fatherhood; that it was the love of the parent for his offspring, of the

Creator for the creature, of the Source of life and being for every measure of life and being, natural and supernatural, in which He has reproduced His own image. With Christ this sense of their derivation and descent from God was ever present; the bond of creaturehood, invisible to other eyes, was visible to His at all times. He beheld the divine love, not merely in its effects and appearances, but in its cause and substance.

Philosophical religion had, at best, argued out some glimmer of the truth, had expressed some such relationship of maker and made, but it had not directly *felt* the love, the Fatherhood. He felt the love, and framed in the love He beheld the truth, intuitively, face to face, without argument. Reason could only oppress men and chill their hearts with the thought of an infinite unlikeness between God and man that made loving relation and intercourse unimaginable. The further it removed men from idols and man-faced deities, the more fatherless it left them.

As reason could not raise God to heaven without taking Him from earth, so neither could the crude religions of the imagination keep Him on earth without dragging Him down from heaven; the more He was for them a Father, the less was He a God. But He whose purity of heart enabled His vision to pierce to the lowest depths and foundations of truth saw the Fatherhood rooted in the Godhead; saw that God was a Father, just because He was God; that He was the nearest, because He was the furthest; the most merciful, because the most just.

No philosophy of God's infinitude and unlikeness could equal the truth implied in Christ's reverence and mystic awe; no fond likeness-making of the imagination could justify or explain His boundless feeling of childlike love and confidence. Reverence and love in Him were fed by no inferences of the mind or pictures of the imagination, but were begotten by direct spiritual contact with the divine; in Him vision, feeling, and will blended together, independent, without priority or succession. This was His spirit; and this was His revelation. The truth that He revealed was Himself; and when He would bequeath us His Truth, He bequeathed us His Spirit, His Love.

4

"He that hath seen Me hath seen the Father." This surely is true, directly, of Christ according to the spirit, not of Christ according to the flesh. It is as a spirit that man is made to be the image of God, who is a spirit. Idolatry sought that divine image in the psychic, natural man; Christ found it in the spiritual man, who is more-than-man, who is the Son of God. Man's spirit is the mirror in which, according to the measure of its purity, God's face is reflected. In One alone were the purity and the reflexion such that He could say without limit: "He that hath seen Me hath seen the Father." Here, as throughout, we speak of Christ's moral and spiritual relation to the Father; not of the metaphysical relation of personal union, which is its mysterious, inscrutable root. We speak of that faultless, unbroken unity of will, which practically merged all distinction of agency and made His spirit-life as much a part of the Divine Life as the life of any member is part of that of the whole body: "The word which ye hear is not Mine, but the Father's who sent Me" (John XIV. 24). "The Son can do nothing of Himself, but what He seeth the Father doing; for what things soever He doeth, these the Son also doeth in like manner" (John V. 19). The spirit feeds on truth; it becomes what it sees. Christ's visible life was purely an expression of His spirit-life; and this again purely an expression of the Divine Life. And thus that Divine Life was made visible: "He that hath seen Me hath seen the Father." In this sense He has taught us that we have a right to look for the likeness of man in God, and for the likeness of God in man: "Face My hands fashioned, see it in Myself!" Thus the blind hankerings of idolatry after a God within the reach of man's mind were tenderly refined and superabundantly satisfied by Him who never yet broke the bruised reed of our mental infirmity, or quenched the smoking flax of our faint desires.

As little as Christ's knowledge of the Father was an inference, so little was His revelation of that knowledge a formula. As He beheld the truth in His love, so He uttered it in His life—in the expression of His love. His life was His doctrine. Reflecting on that life, we try to formulate the truth it implied according to our modes of speech and thought; and thus the Church shapes her theology from age to age. His life and spirit are the subject-matter of this reflection, the supreme rule of faith. His life is the revelation of the Father; of what the Father is in relation to man; of the eternal humanity of God. In Him we see God as a servant in the midst of His creatures, kneeling at their feet, ministering to their needs, feeding them with His flesh and blood, bearing with their infirmities of mind and body, forgiving their sins, healing their sickness; full of compassion for the multitudes; the Friend of publicans and sinners, of simple folk and little children, of the birds of the air and the flowers of the field; the Foe of scribes and Pharisees, of the unreal and pretentious; the upholder of truth and justice and mercy; rejoicing with those that rejoice, as at Cana; weeping with those that weep, as by the tomb of Lazarus; a Good Shepherd who lays down His life for His sheep, yet whom death cannot hold or conquer. "He that hath seen Me hath seen the Father," yet "the Father is greater than I"; for all that He has shown of the Father's humanity, and all that His saints, in whom His spirit continues for ever to develop and unfold its inexhaustible riches, can ever show us is infinitely short of the truth.

5

When complementary truths are set over against one another by some apparent contrariety, owing to the limitation of our outlook, we forget one as we emphasize the other. We are always defective either in our sense of God's nearness or in our sense of His distance; for we only *believe*, where Christ *felt*, and, through feeling, *saw*. Our progress, if we are not to oscillate idly and unprogressively from one side of the truth to the other, demands that in each case we should return to the forgotten side enriched by a deeper realization of the other. In Christ's hearers the sense of God's distance and otherness had been more deeply realized than hitherto. Their more pressing need was to learn that His greatness, far from diminishing, was the measure of His fatherliness; that "the All-Great was the All-Loving too." This Gospel or Good News was for the poor, the lowly, the empty, lest their humility should pass into hopelessness. "Lift up your heads, for your redemption draweth nigh"—such was its burden. If our Saviour preached the love, He also preached the greatness, in order to measure and enhance the love: "You call Me the Lord and Master; you say well, for so I am.... I, your Lord and Master, wash your feet." God, who on earth washed their feet, through Him, was not only their Father, but their Father *in heaven*.

Heaven for Christ's hearers meant God's dwelling-place above the sky, from whence He viewed the world beneath and governed it through the ministry of ascending and descending angels. Our own conceptions of the Beyond are not so adequate that we can afford to set these simpler and more confident representations aside as religiously valueless. In one point we may easily underrate them, through our inability to clothe ourselves in the garment of the past. If our astronomy has in some way enlarged, it has also impoverished, our notion of the heavens. It has given us quantitative mysteries in exchange for qualitative; it has made heaven homogeneous with earth. The once mysterious planets, and the sun itself, are but material orbs like our own; and as the mind travels endlessly into space it meets only with more orbs and systems of orbs in their millions, an infinite monotony of matter and motion, but never does it strike against some boundary wall of the universe, beyond which God keeps an eternal Sabbath in a new order of existence, a mysterious world which eye has not seen, nor ear heard, nor heart conceived. The heaven that lay behind the blue curtain of the sky, whence night by night God hung out His silver lamps to shine upon the earth, was a far deeper symbol of the eternal home than the cold, shelterless deserts of astronomical space.

For the Galilean fishermen, heaven stood for distance and transcendence, for a world other in kind than our our—however imperfectly they may have grasped the extent of that otherness. The expression "Father in Heaven," or "Heavenly Father," reminded them of difference as well as of likeness, and warned them that they were on holy ground and in the region of mystery.

This sense of God's otherness, unlikeness, infinitude is, both historically and philosophically, of the very essence of religion—the motive of that reverence, awe, and worship, which is even a more primary element than love, confidence, and sonship. Man passes from the religion of servitude and fear to that of liberty and the Gospel; yet he does not leave fear behind, but carries it on with him, deepened and spiritualized, into a reverence that is part of the very substance of love.

Christ's reverential love was that of one to whom earth was permeated by heaven as by an all-pervading ether invisible to less pure eyes than His own. The enfolding curtain of the sky was for Him but a symbol of the manner in which the visible and material is encompassed and penetrated by the spiritual. It was not from beyond the outmost circumference of space that He sought the explanation and source of all that exists and lives and moves; but in the very centre of each several creature, living in its life, breathing in its breath, yet transcending it infinitely in kind and nature. For Him earth and heaven were continuous, as the light and heat of the sun. The visible, of itself meaningless, found its complement and explanation in the invisible, as a part is explained when the whole is revealed. For Him the whole realm of ruthless law and necessity was but an instrument in the grasp of liberty and love which, without destroying its structure, could bend it to their own designs. The world of matter was but a little islet afloat on the boundless, encompassing ocean of spirit, rising and falling on its bosom, borne hither and thither by its currents, yet held together within itself by rigid relations of necessity. With seeming indifference the sun might rise upon the evil and the good, the rain descend upon the just and the unjust, the sparrows whom Nature had nursed might fall to the ground, the grass she had clothed with glory might wither and fade, but behind all and over all were the love and care of the Heavenly Father.

6

Man's heart has always been too big for earth to fill, too hungry to be satisfied with the mere husks of reality. Repressed again and again by various sorts of materialism, the mystic appetite as often reasserts itself, and will feed on any garbage if wholesome food be denied it. A world of rigid law and order, a world of blind chance and chaos, are alike intolerable to a spiritual being, which necessarily seeks its own likeness at the root of things, and will be satisfied with nothing less, while ready to accept infinitely more.

We must, then, recognize a perverted truth and value in the crude mysticism which dreams of a divine power alongside of and, in some sense, co-ordinate with nature, as a ruler is co-ordinate with his subjects; a power which the powers of nature, in the main, obey according to prescribed laws, and whose existence is only revealed when it breaks through this order of nature and comes into collision with it. Mysticism of this kind looks for God, not in order but in disorder, in storms and earthquakes and portents, in abnormal states and phenomena of the spiritual faculties, in seeming disturbances of nature's rhythm that point to the intervention of a will above nature. Yet so steadily and persistently does maturer knowledge tend to reduce these seeming exceptions to some higher rule, that to build our divinity solely on such foundations is to build it on the sand. He to whose spiritual gaze nature was transparent has taught us the true mysticism; He has taught us to see God, not alongside of nature, but to see nature in the bosom of God, and God through and in nature; to find Him as revealed in the rule; to seek for Him as hidden in the exception; to believe in a unity which we cannot yet see; to hope in a love which we cannot yet understand. There can be no conflict of faith and science when faith compasses science as heaven compasses earth; when mysteries are sought not in the faults and lacunas of science, but in the higher world that permeates and engulfs the visible order, in the darkness from which it comes and into which it vanishes, a darkness which faith alone can enlighten.

7

Like a water-weed, whose blossom alone floats on the surface, man's being is, for the most part, merged in the spiritual world and reaches up to the visible order only in virtue of its psychic and organic manifestations. Slight as may be the seen indications of his connexion with the hidden, they are there nevertheless. To bring them to full consciousness, to control his psychic life entirely by that consciousness, is the work of religion. The spirit-life, as we have said, is that in which a man's interests have been so identified with the divine, universal interest that he becomes dead to himself, to his narrow, separate, psychic self, and feels that God has taken possession of him, that he is merely an instrument of the Divine Will: "I live, yet not I, but Christ liveth in me." It means a disinterested devotion to truth in every form—truth of life, truth of feeling, truth of vision. In virtue of this spirit-life man belongs (actually, to some degree; potentially, to an indefinite degree) to heaven rather than to earth, for he is a son of the Heavenly Father, the " Father of Spirits." Heaven is his home, his natural environment; it is the communion of all wills, so far as they are identified with the divine, and through the divine with one another; it is the Invisible Church, the Communion of Saints.

It is hell, and not earth, that is described in the Gospel as separated from heaven by an impassable gulf. A view of heaven that would so cut it off from earth would turn earth into hell: "Where Thou art," says à Kempis, "there is heaven; and where Thou art not, there is hell." As the spiritual order enwraps and permeates the physical and makes with it one intelligible unity, so the spiritual and psychic in man are not, by right, antagonistic or mutually exclusive, but belong to the same whole. What God hath joined together, let no man put asunder. In this truth we stand firm against all false asceticism as against all false mysticism. The height of heaven above earth is not local but qualitative; a distance of kind, not of space; a distance that no more stands in the way of unity and nearness than the distance that separates the spirit from the body which it informs, and which it could not possibly inform were it like in kind.

8

Christ has "given us power to become the sons of God." This gift or grace supposes a certain

receptivity in us which belongs to us as spiritual
beings. A merely psychic being could not so much
as desire or receive the gift. It is difficult and idle
to speculate what man would be without grace;
without that perpetual "giving" on God's side, apart
from which our spirit-life would remain purely
dormant. It is of God's gift that the last and
least of us from time to time rises above the psychic
self and elicits some disinterested act of goodness.
It is of His gift that we desire to multiply such acts,
and to sustain ourselves continuously on the spiritual
level. It is of His gift that we weary of the psychic
self-seeking life; that we cry out against our limitations; that we ask and seek and knock: "Thou
wouldst not have sought Me, if thou hadst not
already found Me." All that the merely psychic
man can do of himself is to work out his own
misery; to learn by some wider experience the
hollowness of the highest attainment of the lower
non-spiritual life. So far and no further can he
"prepare himself for grace," unawares—wandering,
as it were, into a far country with his face turned
from home. To realize that he is not enough for
himself, that he needs another, that Other must first
present Himself to him in his loneliness; must run
to meet him. Unlike the monologue of the ethical
life, the spirit-life is essentially a converse, a com-
munication, a passing out of self into God; it is an
affair between two; a mutual giving and receiving.
Without grace it is unthinkable. The initiative
must be from God; as it is with all life. It is He
who "teaches us to pray," who gives us the desire to

pray; to arise and go to our Father. It is by prayer that we strain forward to meet Him; that we open our arms to receive the kiss of peace; that we stretch out our hands for the ring and the robe. It is by the "raising of the heart and mind to God," by the spiritualizing of our affections and thoughts, that through grace we make ourselves sons of God.

This Divine Life is not something that we draw forth from ourselves, but rather something that we appropriate. To be a spirit is simply to have the power of appropriating it when it is offered to us. We might say this in some measure of the civilization into which we are born; of that organized system of beliefs, traditions, customs, and institutions which society has slowly built up. This, too, is a ready-made life which the individual may appropriate and enter into. If he would stand alone he must remain on the brute level, a savage at best. Still more, the Divine Life—God's mind, God's love, God's will—is something which the Spirit lays hold of and appropriates in various measures; which it cannot educe from itself, and for which it is as dependent on God as the babe is on its mother.

Being Himself in the fullest possession of this spirit-life, and imparting it to us, Christ has given us power to become the sons of God. He is Himself the bread of that life; and in the measure that we feed on Him we become what He is.

9

It was in the consciousness of union and solidarity with his people past and present, of membership in

Israel, that the Jew invoked God as "our Father." He was Israel's God, the God of Abraham, Isaac, and Jacob. Moab and Egypt had their gods; but Israel alone had the true God, and none could claim His fatherhood and protection save through Israel and as adopted into the family of Abraham. There was a note of exclusiveness in the pronoun "our"; it meant "ours and not theirs." That the individual as such and apart from his title of membership with Israel had a right to call God "Father" or "my Father" had hardly come into clear and general recognition in Christ's day. As in earlier forms of society, the people was everything, the individual was altogether subordinate. Israel collectively was God's son, or if later the dignity was vested in the King or the promised Messias, it was as in the representative of the whole people.

It is to the influence of Christ's teaching that we owe that development of the sense of personality which has destroyed the excessive collectivity of ancient social institutions, has led to a juster idea of the relation of the individual to the community, and has taught us that neither can be wholly subordinated to the other; that their interests are common; that the hurt and perfection of the one is the hurt and perfection of the other. But the modern reaction against old-world collectivism has often been in the direction of a crude individualism, as hurtful to true spiritual personality as ever was slavery. One great factor at least of such personality was saved in the Israelite's sense of participation in a corporate life, in the cause of God, in the Kingdon of Heaven.

When he stood in the temple with the worshippers, when he went forth to fight the battles of Israel, he was no longer himself in the narrow sense; it was the life of God's people which pulsed in his veins and raised him to the over-individual level. He had not yet realized his own separate value and importance in the eyes of Him who is the Father of each as well as the Father of all: he had not yet broken down the walls of partition that divided Israel after the flesh from Israel after the spirit, that narrowed the cause of God to the cause of a nation; he had not yet entered into an all-inclusive universal life, but he had to a great extent risen to a sense of spiritual personality and had entered into the Divine Life as far as he understood it.

Far deeper and wider was the divine love that burned in Christ's heart, and whose meaning and implication was ever clear to His vision. He who felt not merely the effects and manifestations of God's fatherliness towards Israel, but also its very root and substance, felt also that it could not be so limited to Israel as to exclude any creature begotten and sustained by the Eternal Love; that though there were infinite degrees and kinds of sonship, yet God's love for the least of His children was "greater than the measure of man's mind"; that no will could be perfectly true to His which set limits to human brotherhood. It is not the voice of Israel alone, but the voice of all humanity, the voice of all creation, the blended voices of the "Benedicite," that cried, "Our Father who art in heaven."

This is evident from our Lord's whole practice and

teaching as set before us in the Gospels, and as interpreted more explicitly by St. Paul. His life was one prolonged fight against exclusivism in any sense; and in the interests of Catholicism in every sense. Whom or what did He shut out from His love? Nothing that bears the shape of man; nothing that breathes the breath of life; not the birds of the air, nor the grass of the field, nor the heaven that is God's throne, nor the earth that is His footstool. Hence St. Paul (Col. I. 19) speaks of the whole fulness of creation as dwelling in Him, as gathered up into His consciousness and His love, as already sharing in the redemption which His blood had wrought for all mankind, as groaning and travailling for the fuller deliverance to come.

10

This sense of solidarity, through God, with all that proceeds from God and belongs to God, is of the essence of the spirit-life. "All things are yours; and you are Christ's, and Christ is God's." God is transcendent; He stretches beyond the world in every direction; infinitely higher, deeper, wider. But it is only through, in, and with the world that we are one with Him; we must take it all into ourselves, into our thought, feeling, and will, if we would possess Him. That mysticism is doomed to sterility which would seek Him, like the entombed hermits of Thibet, in absolute silence and darkness, which would empty the mind and heart of every creature in the vain hope of finding more room for God. As little could our mind think of life apart from things that live. What God is out of relation to His creatures, His creatures can never know. Whatever ghostly figure of Him such abstract contemplation may conjure up owes the little substance it has to relics of concrete living experience which the mind has failed to banish, and which still cling to it in its mad endeavour to soar up beyond all atmosphere to the region of the Absolute.

The seeming justification of this endeavour to escape from creatures lies in the notorious fact that the preoccupation and overcrowding of the heart and mind with creatures is manifestly hurtful to converse with God. Such converse is favoured by the liberation of the faculties for the contemplation of divine things; hence the conclusion that a total liberation should be our aim. This is equivalent to supposing that because surfeit is injurious to health, starvation can never hurt us. Life, experience, is the pabulum of the spirit. As the bee goes to and fro between the garden and its hive, now gathering, now storing up and utilizing what it has gathered, so the spirit lives by alternations of experience and reflection. An undue excess of either over the other is fatal; either religion is choked amid thorns and briars, or it becomes abstract, empty, unreal, out of relation to life, a frail thought-structure imperilled by every breath of fresh air. We need then to pause frequently in life; to turn from experience back to reflection and prayer, so as to consider experience explicitly in its relation to God as revealing Him; and then to turn from prayer and reflection to the quest of new experience with an enlarged capacity for receiving and profiting by it; with a greater power of assimilating it. And thus gradually the whole world should become food to us. "If thy heart were but right," says à Kempis, "every creature would be to thee a mirror of life, a holy book; for there is no creature so small or despicable as not in some way to represent the divine goodness." The way to contemplation, therefore, is not to fly from creatures, but so to rectify the heart by reflection that one can gradually embrace them all; for the more we embrace of them, the more we embrace of God.

The spirit in prayer then comes face to face with God without intermediary; but it must not come alone, isolated, separate. Such separateness belongs to the psychic self. The spirit takes the whole world into its thought and affection; gives it a consciousness and a voice which cries, not "My Father," but "Our Father"—"ours," because inclusive of everything, exclusive of nothing. Through the spirit the whole world returns to God in praise; but to return through it the world must first enter into it; must be assimilated and transformed by it.

In One alone has it been so perfectly; that One whose "heart was right" in an unique sense; that One who alone could say, "All Mine are Thine, and all Thine are Mine"; that One in whom "it pleased the Father that all fulness should dwell," and of whose fulness we have all received.

II

It is, then, vain to approach the altar, to draw near to God if one is estranged from one's brother. Let him first go, and by reconciliation take the whole world into his heart and so come and offer it, together with himself, as a gift. As the negative estrangement of indifference starves the soul, and as the positive estrangement of hostility narrows and contracts it by pressure and opposition, so it is sustained, strengthened, expanded, enriched by spiritual communion with others, in the measure that it lives in them and they in it. "I in them, and Thou in Me, that we all may be perfect in one."

If this holds pre-eminently of the "rational creature," i.e. of the world of spirits and wills, yet it must be extended in due proportion to the humbler and humblest orders of existence to which man, in virtue of his complex nature, stands in relation of brotherhood—

> He prayeth best who loveth best
>   All things both great and small ;
> For the dear God who loveth us,
>   He made and loveth all.

This we had learnt already from the Hebrew psalmist; this was the inspiration of the authors of the *Laudate* and the *Benedicite*. But what with them may have been but a spiritual instinct, was for Christ a felt fact, a clear vision. His joy in creation was enriched with a sense of fraternity and affection. He beheld all things proceeding from the same root as man, fostered by the same love. It was the same Father who clothed the lilies of the field and Solomon in all his glory; who fed the birds of the air and the Israelites in the desert; who noted the fall of a sparrow and numbered the hairs of man's head. To the Poverello of Assisi belongs the glory of having resolved the harmony of Christ's spirit into its closely allied components of sorrow and joy; of having taken each apart, and brought it home with new freshness to the Christian consciousness. The prophets had told us that "the sea is His, and He made it, and His hands prepared the dry land: the strength of the hills is His also"; that "the earth is the Lord's, and the fulness thereof"; that "sun, moon, and stars obey Him"; that "the winds are His messengers and the lightnings His ministers"; but they had hardly reached that joyous sense of brotherhood and friendliness which belongs to the child of God and springs from the deeper intuition of His Fatherhood, which greets the sun as a brother, and the moon as a sister, through an inspiration of true fraternal feeling and not merely through a flight of poetic fancy.

It may be rightly objected that this nature-feeling often exists when the love of God and man is weak, and is absent when this is strong. One might reply that those who so lack it would be all the better for it; that those who possess it would be still worse without it; that no one loves God more for loving nature less; or less for loving nature more. The true answer is that not all nature-feeling is religious, but only that which springs from the intuition of God's Fatherhood, and whose quality and extent are determined by the depth and purity of that intuition.

12

"Generationem ejus quis enarrabit?"—"Who shall declare His generation?" These words have been applied somewhat uncritically by patristic writers to signify the mysterious generation of the Eternal Son. They might be applied with equal truth to the mystery of the origin of all things; to the relation of fatherhood and sonship that obtains between God and the last and least of His creatures. We know well that the dependence of the creature is immeasurably greater, closer, and other than that of a son; that sonship is little more than a symbol, a feeble image of the reality, an expression which belongs to the order of parables and similitudes rather than to that of allegories or metaphors. We cannot break the idea into its factors, and find for each of them a parallel in the relation of creaturehood. Some of them correspond, others do not; hence sonship is a similitude of creaturehood, partly like, partly unlike. Thus a son is begotten by an act that passes, but a creature is being breathed forth by God's love at every moment of its existence; a son becomes separate from and independent of his father, but a creature is ever clinging to the bosom of God; a son is a product of blind instinct and necessity, but a creature is a product of intelligence and unconstrained love; a son reaches maturity and attains the perfection of his father's nature, but a creature will always fall infinitely short of the perfection of the Creator. Other relationships offer points of similitude, and have been used to supplement the poverty of that of fatherhood and sonship. "Though a mother should forget her child, yet will not I forget thee." "How often would I have gathered thee as a hen gathereth her chickens under her wing." "There is One that sticketh closer than a brother." "Abraham was called the friend of God." Here we see how God is our mother, brother, and friend. Mystics delight to see in Him the soul's Spouse and Lover. Nay, He is even in some way the child of His children; the servant of His servants: "Inasmuch as ye did it to the least of these My little ones, ye did it unto Me." "Lo! I am in your midst as he who serveth"—for our Lord says these things in the name of the Father and as revealing the Father, who in so many ways is dependent on us and serves us.

Yet fatherhood is the similitude in which He has principally revealed His relation to us. And if in various civilizations the rights and duties of fatherhood have been variously understood, we need not on that account be over-critical to determine exactly how they were understood in Galilee 2,000 years ago; for that would be to press a similitude point by point as though it were a metaphor. Its value lies in what fatherhood signifies everywhere and always, under all varieties of usage and custom, namely, a claim to reverence and love.

13

The conception of God as a father is easy for religion in its childish stages, when reverence and love are but crude and embryonic. But when science has pulverized the earth and made it a speck in a measureless waste of suns; when it has shown us the reign of ruthless law in little and great, outside us and within us; and when reflection has penetrated us with the sense of God's otherness and unlikeness and brought it home to our feeling and imagination —then, indeed, it is only the very heroism of faith that can affirm a likeness and sameness notwithstanding, and can say, "Our Father who art in heaven." Yet without such faith, our mental and moral life must be brought to a standstill through a paralysing scepticism. If God's otherness were such that what is false for us might be true for Him, or what is evil in us might be good in Him; if, as rash preachers have sometimes implied, He has a right to deceive or to be cruel; if differences of false and true, good and evil, depend merely on His arbitrary *fiat*—then our standards of moral and mental endeavour are purely relative. We might fear such a Being as we fear an earthquake, or a volcano, or the unknown and capricious forces of nature; but reverence Him we could not. Reverence is not of the merely vast and wondrous, but of an excellence that is vast and wonderful; what we reverence is an excellence which we can imagine, magnified beyond our imagination. And this excellence is that of personality, of the human spirit—its power, wisdom, goodness, and love. In us, these attributes are separate, and limited each of its kind; that in God they should be unlimited and identical makes Him endlessly vast and wonderful, the supreme object of mystic awe. It makes Him unlike us in His likeness. But it is the substance of these same spiritual excellences, as distinct from their limits and modes, that makes Him like us in His unlikeness, and constrains us to cry, "Our Father."

But it is only by faith of the highest kind that this Fatherhood can be held firmly, so as to be the governing inspiration of our lives. The evidence of all-controlling goodness and love in the world round us grows weaker and not stronger in the cold light of purely intellectual criticism; for such criticism excludes the reasons of the heart. It sees only a vast mechanism, callously grinding out good and evil, joy and sorrow, on no conceivable plan; now rewarding virtue, now punishing it, with a capriciousness that excludes all idea of intelligent goodness. We could not possibly love, praise, or reverence a man who acted as nature, or God through nature, often seems to act. We should feel ourselves immeasurably better than such a one, for all our selfishness and frailty—that is to say, if we were to attend to what *seems* to be; to the imperfect revelation of God given in the world, apart from the things made known in the heart. Could the worst of us stand by and witness the agonies of any innocent, reasonless creature, child or animal, if our bare *fiat* could relieve those agonies? One such instance would be an unanswerable difficulty against millions of contrary instances. Yet there are oceans of such seemingly gratuitous and useless agony all round us at every moment. We cannot, then, under pain of moral scepticism, say that the world, as it seems in the light of purely intellectual criticism, appears to be the work of One who is at once all-good and all-mighty.

But to study the world apart from man's heart is like studying music on its mathematical side and without reference to the ear. Man's heart is also the heart of the world, not something outside it; and neither of them can be studied truthfully in abstraction from the other. Had the Bouddha looked within as well as without, he might have divined a power that could transmute the all-pervading waters of human tribulation into the wine of gladness; but in his contemplation he sat aloof, as one who witnesses a play in which he has no part; as having no sense of his solidarity with the world which he condemned.

Faith in God's Fatherhood is our answer to the revelation of His Fatherhood, a revelation which is made in our own spirit by God's Spirit. It comes to us as a feeling, not as a blind feeling, but as a felt truth, a felt reality; as a feeling which implies and demands a truth. "We have received the spirit of adoption wherein we cry, Abba, Father." "The Spirit itself beareth witness to our spirit that we are the Sons of God." And, in its ethical manifestation, this Spirit is "Charity" or "Love." It is therefore in the sudden kindling of our purest and strongest spiritual love that the revelation of God's Fatherhood is given to our faith; when "Like a man in wrath, the heart stands up and answers, 'I have felt'"; when it asks: "Shall man be more just than his Maker?" "Shall he be more good, more pitiful, more wise, more loving?" "He that made the eye, shall He not see? He that made the ear, shall He not hear? He that made the heart, shall He not understand?" In such moments we feel that the life and the love within us stream from the very centre and heart of reality, from the veins of the Eternal who lives in us, who is our Father in heaven; we feel that what pains and resists our higher will in the world around us, pains and resists Him too; that He through us and in us, in some mysterious way, is in conflict with all that evil whose opposition to the spirit is the very condition of our spiritual growth and expansion; that in us He is battling with ignorance, error, selfishness, suffering, and sin.

It is this faith in the revelation of the spirit, faith in the intuitions of love, faith in the felt truths of our best moments, that warms and fills up the chill and ghostly conception of a "Supreme Being," infinitely vast and strange, that corrects our despairing sense of God's otherness and distance by a trustful sense of His likeness and nearness; that transforms mere awe and wonder into filial reverence and love.

Of this faith it is said: "No man knoweth the Son but the Father; neither knoweth any man the Father save the Son and he to whom the Son will reveal Him."

14

This explicit faith in God's Fatherhood gives life its warmth. Let us contrast the life without faith in its best and highest manifestation, and the life with faith in its thinnest and poorest manifestation. Let us take the case of a truly cultivated man of the highest moral principle and practice, one whose will is, unawares, altogether sympathetic with the Divine Will, whose life is sincerely, selflessly, and enthusiastically devoted to the interests of truth and goodness, and yet whose religion has remained implicit and latent; who has never realized the Lawgiver behind the law which his conscience imposes; who has never felt the personality of that Goodness and Truth for whose claims he would utterly sacrifice self indeed, but with a confused notion that it was himself to whom he was sacrificing. Such a purely ethical life (so far as explicit consciousness goes) is after all a monologue of the heart, a cold soliloquy. The faith that somehow or other Goodness matters absolutely and eternally, is a blind faith that must either stumble, or open its eyes on God's face. As the race of man on earth began, so it will also end within an appreciable time; and then, faith apart, what will it matter whether we have lived well or ill? Is not, then, the affirmation of conscience as to the absolute and eternal importance of right a lie? Only by a studious self-blinding to ultimate problems can such a man as we have described escape a sterilizing pessimism, and maintain his spirit-life in its vigour. And even if he succeed, still in his heart he is always alone.

And if, as usually happens, the circumstances and conditions are far less favourable than above described; if he be an uncultured, lonely, aimless, unsuccessful or much-tempted man, then he will feel the chill of faithlessness far more keenly than one clad in prosperity. But let a man be never so impoverished and obscure socially, mentally, and even morally, if he has an explicit faith in God's Fatherhood, it will transform his spirit-life into a dialogue, and abolish his inward loneliness. Each thought and action, however small, is felt not only to matter absolutely and eternally, but to strengthen or loosen ties of love and friendship with the Divine Spirit and Father of Spirits.

"I am not alone," says Christ, "but I, and the Father who sent Me" (John VIII. 16). If a certain dualism of oneself against oneself is a practical necessity of the moral life, a dualism of person against person is no less a necessity of the religious life; and to this need He has ministered who taught us to say, "Our Father."

15

Thus the new wine bursts the old bottles. The new love of Christ, the new commandment of Christ, the new spirit of Christ, could not be cramped up in the Old Testament categories and modes of thought. Into every time-honoured phrase and expression a new wealth of meaning was crowded. "Go, borrow thee vessels abroad of all thy neighbours, even empty vessels; borrow not a few" (2 Kings IV. 3). In obedience to some such prophetic impulse the Christian Church wandered forth among the Gentiles, borrowing their vessels, even their empty vessels, right and left, to hold the treasures for which she found no receptacle in the home of her birth. And if the flow of oil is stayed, it is not that its source is dry, or that we have exhausted the depth of meaning latent in the "Our

Father," but only because "there is not a vessel more." Whenever human thought frames a larger and worthier vessel, that too will be filled.

Christ's love was a "felt truth"; feeling alone was its adequate expression; no language could ever equal it. It was not only the feeling of a truth, but the feeling of an end, of a will to be accomplished; it was at once a perfection of mind, heart, and will—of the whole spirit-life.

The invocation, "Our Father who art in heaven," is designed to bring our spirit into accord with His; to determine our inward attitude of prayer in the presence of God; to adjust our feeling, our thought, and our will; to safeguard the emotional, moral, and mystical interests of the spirit against mutual encroachments, against Sentimentality, against Mysticality, and against Practicality.

IV

THE FIRST PETITION

Sanctificetur Nomen tuum.—Hallowed be Thy Name

I

It has been suggested that these words embody an aspiration, like "Alleluia" or "Blessed be God," rather than a formal prayer or petition, and that as such they belong to the invocation preceding the petitions. No doubt analogies favouring this view abound in Hebrew liturgy and psalmody. Yet not only has the constant tradition of the Church numbered this among the petitions, but the difference between aspiration and petition in such a case is superficial and not substantial. Viewed as an aspiration, "Blessed be God" is a wish; viewed as a petition, it is an appeal to Heaven for the realization of that wish. It is the substance of the wish that concerns us. What child of God could wish and not also pray and work for the hallowing of His Name? Moreover, the petitions of the Lord's Prayer are justly considered as a summary of the principal aims of our Saviour's life and work upon earth; and of these the hallowing of His Father's Name was among the first: "I have glorified Thee on earth. . . . I have manifested Thy Name." The Christian's first aim should be the Christian's first prayer. Also it is noticeable that St. Luke, who keeps to the barest substance of the prayer and reduces the invocation to the word "Father" (which St. Matthew amplifies), retains the clause in question, which he would hardly do were it a mere embellishment. But, at best, the point is academic, and need not detain us.

2

A prayer of petition involves feeling, vision, and will, and thus brings the whole spirit into exercise or act. It implies a wish or desire, born of a perceived contrast between what we are and might be, between what we have and might have; and also a will to give effect to and satisfy the said wish, to change the sense of hunger into a sense of fruition.

This holds of prayer in its simplest and most self-seeking form, of the prayer which the psychic or natural man pours forth to the gods whom he seeks to control in his own interest as he would control the forces of nature; gods whom he has often confounded with those same forces; gods whom he serves only that they may serve him; who are to him as means, not as ends; the most powerful of his friends, the most dangerous of his foes.

Far different is the petition of the spirit, and born of a diviner discontent; for it is the prayer that God Himself prays in man, the cry of a Will in us that is divine—our own, yet not our own. Friendship makes us forget our own particular interest in the particular interest of another; makes us see with his eyes, feel with his feelings, will with his will; but the prayer that raises our heart and mind to God by way of likeness and conformity, makes us forget our own particular interest in an interest that is divine and universal. If this now becomes "my" interest, yet it is in no exclusive sense, but only because my will has been so perfectly merged in God's and made one with it that "mine" and "His" are the same: "All mine are Thine and all Thine are mine."

This discontent of the spirit is a divine discontent; it is God's own discontent; it is His knowledge of the contrast of the actual with the ideal; of things as they are with things as they ought to be; of the little good accomplished with the much that has yet to be accomplished—it is this knowledge as in some measure communicated to us and felt by us. And out of this divine feeling and will is begotten in us a will to remedy our spiritual discontent, to devote ourselves entirely to the task.

The sense that this desire and will though in us is not of us, that it is an impulse and direction received from One in whose hands we are voluntary instruments, carries with it a sense that the work is not principally our own but His; that it is altogether beyond our unassisted powers; that our efficiency depends on our acknowledging our dependence, and in adapting ourselves in everything to the hand that wields us so as to follow its impulse and direction as faithfully as possible. Not only must we pray as well as work, but we must pray precisely in order that we may have the desire and will to work; for it is by prayer that we dispose ourselves to the influence of the Divine Will, subjecting and adjusting ourselves to the hand that moves and guides us. Nor is implicit prayer enough: but we must from time to time withdraw our attention from our work and turn it upon our relation to God, so as to readjust whatever may have gone amiss or may lessen the energy or accuracy of our aim. We pray, then, not merely that God's will may be accomplished, but above all that we ourselves may will to work for its accomplishment.

3

We pray, then, that we may be filled with God's Will as to the hallowing of His Name; that He may stir us up to desire and work for this end.

To the Galilean disciples the words will have had, *mutatis mutandis*, much the same suggestion as for ourselves. God's Name stood to them for man's notion or knowledge of God; for that representation of Him by which He is made present to the human mind. Israel might make no graven image of Jehovah, but to the sacred Name itself an external honour was paid—not strange in times when even a man's name was held to be almost part of himself, impregnated with his spirit and power, expressive of his nature and destiny, something through which he could be controlled and affected even in his absence. Idea and thing, name and idea, were far closer wedded in those days than in our own. But even when Christ spoke, the hallowing of God's Name had, for popular religious consciousness, little suggestion of the mere external honour of taboo. It meant, as it means for us, the upholding of God's honour and glory in the esteem of men. The son holds the father's repute as his own. The reputation of Israel and of the God of Israel were one and the same thing. The dishonour of one was the dishonour of the other: "Not unto us, O Lord, not unto us, but unto Thy Name give glory; lest perchance the Gentiles say, Where is now their God?"

In the measure that religion rose above the psychic to the spiritual plane, and that the interests of truth and right were felt to be absolute, to be not only above individual interests, but above those of the Jewish nation itself—this identification of God's honour with Israel's needed careful limitation lest the son should bring shame upon the Father and tarnish the glory of His holy Name. This was the fear that kindled the zeal and indignation of the prophets, according as they beheld God mirrored more clearly in the purity of their own hearts and contrasted that image of His glory with the travesty frequently offered to men's eyes by the life, practice, and teaching of Israel, His son and appointed representative.

It was to this representative and exponent that the alien or even the individual Israelite was taught to look for his conception of the Divine Will and Character; it was through this glass, so often blurred and stained, that the pure light of heaven had to reach his eye. If, owing to the limits of the human mind, some such mediation was a necessity, surely it was also a danger; nor could any idol, however grotesque and unworthy, libel the Divinity more effectually than the false lives and false teaching of the living representation. Thus what should be a gate of access became a barrier of separation: the window of light was made into a curtain of darkness. Israel was to the world what the eye is to the body: " The lamp of the body is the eye; if thine eye be single, thy whole body shall be full of light; but if thine eye be evil, thy whole body shall be full of darkness." God had "put His Name in Israel," He had committed His honour on earth to the safe keeping of his people, and thereby exposed it to endless fluctuations and mischances. Yet in His saints and prophets He had provided for the continual correction and elevation of the public representation of His Name. It was no lifeless impress graven with a style upon rock, but was written only too delibly in the heart of Israel and liable to be falsified and obliterated were not the letters renewed and deepened day by day through the ministry of the prophetic spirit.

4

The fulness of truth beyond all prophetic insight as to the Divine Nature, and as to God's Fatherhood, was involved in the love that burned in Christ's heart, wherein vision and feeling were blended as are the sun's light and glow. None realized as He the infinite difference that must always obtain between the Name of God, between any possible human conception or representation of His Fatherhood, and the ineffable reality which the name Father symbolizes. Yet also, being man, He knew too well what was in man not to realize how essential this naming of the Unnamable is for the waking and development of man's spiritual life. Not that any naming of God, or notioning of God, will of itself make Him known to the heart by inward experience; but that such inward experience is occasioned, fixed, communized, and fostered by such naming. For association and converse with others is the indispensable condition of any sort of development of the spirit-life; and such converse with others involves the understanding and naming of our experience. Nay, even for the inward converse and soliloquy of the soul, which is so needful for the unfolding and fertilizing of its capacities, notions and names are requisite. To shut out the understanding from all participation in the spiritual life, to trust merely to intuition or to the implicit apprehension involved in feeling and love, would be to exclude the normal condition of yet deeper love and wider intuition; it would be to embrace a false mysticism that divides the spirit and impoverishes the fulness of its life. Man is not *only* a "reasoning animal," but he is nevertheless a reasoning animal. The reasons of the head are not his only reasons, but neither are the reasons of the heart. It is not enough to feel God, to apprehend Him implicitly in the love by which He is really present in us; we must also name Him; and name Him as worthily as we can. "Sanctificetur Nomen tuum."

5

To admit this is to admit the rights of theology; for the naming of God is the beginning and root of all theology. "A faith that really springs out of our rational or spiritual nature, or commends itself to it, cannot be fundamentally irrational or incapable of being explained and defended; and a reason which is unable to find an intelligible meaning in some of the deepest experiences of human souls must be one-sided and imperfectly developed."[1] In other words, there must be reflection on religious experience as on all other experience if it is not to be squandered.

Between the theology and the spiritual life of the Church there is a process of action and reaction necessary for the development of both. The former increases our command of the latter, and every such increase of religious experience entails a widening and readjustment of our theological conceptions. "Never has there been a religious experience without some sort of connected notions as to the relations of

[1] "The Evolution of Theology in the Greek Philosophers," by Ed. Caird, vol. I, p. 20.

Self, God, and the World, i.e. without dogmas. Dogmas are the presupposition of every religious experience which forthwith utters and fixes itself in new dogmas. There never has been an undogmatic Christianity, nor ever can be. Not only does a religious experience, owing to the essential connexion between the understanding and the other functions of the spirit-life, of necessity seek to utter itself in dogmas, but it is itself the offspring of a religious disposition which is fixed by dogma."[1]

These purely philosophical conclusions of non-Catholic thinkers are worth noting at a time when a well-merited reaction against the excesses of intellectualism in the past bids fair to hurry us into the arms of sentimentalism and mysticality: when, lest we should be content to name God without feeling Him, we are often advised to be content to feel Him without naming Him. What we need is to recognize the value of both, and their true relation to one another; to be content with neither alone, nor yet to confound them. Certainly it would be great folly to confound Physical Science with Physical Nature, our abstract system of names and notions with the inexhaustible ever-growing body of experience which it symbolizes and represents. Yet we do not despise our scientific structure because it has to be continually broken up and reconstituted so as to correspond to new tracts of experience which it has itself brought within our reach. We know it is the barest algebra of reality, meaningless for any-

[1] Wilhelm Dilthey, "Naturliches System der Geisterwissenschäften im 17 Jahrh." Archiv f. Gesch. d. Philos. VI, s. 370.

one to whom the experience-value of its signs were unknown, yet it is an instrument of priceless importance through which experience has been brought under man's control, and the possibilities of life have been enlarged in every direction. Science multiplies and deepens experience; experience so multiplied bursts through the categories of science and demands its reform: and so each aids and furthers the other.

So, too, with the naming of God and the experiencing of God in the spiritual life of the world; theology and devotion act and react upon each other, and whoever would vainly strive to petrify one or the other would show no understanding of the process. Let our name or notion of God, the system of our theological ideas, be petrified irreformably, and all further religious experience is sterilized and squandered for lack of dogmatic expression and record; the name of God from being a help to the experience of God becomes a hindrance; through the alteration and growth of its object the representation becomes a misrepresentation. Identified with such a misrepresentation, God becomes for us unreal and even unlovable. Hence, while acknowledging the close connexion between God and His Name, we must take care never to identify them, or to forget that He is infinitely greater and better than any thought of Him we can frame; that in His Name we have only His abstract representation, but that in the love which He kindles in our hearts by His Holy Spirit we have His real presence. This clearly understood, we cannot pray or work too hard for the hallowing of His Name, for the continual perfection of a representation always imperfect, always short of the Living Truth, always susceptible of perfection in the measure that the Living Truth reveals itself to religious experience.

6

But besides the laboured language of theology which clothes the conceptions of the understanding, there is the inspired language of revelation which clothes the intuitions of the heart, and in which religious experience embodies itself so spontaneously as to become almost visible and incarnate. Theology tells us God is Self-existent, infinite, eternal; Revelation tells us He is our Father; Theology expresses the mind's conception of His goodness, Revelation expresses the heart's feeling and experience of His goodness. Though intimately connected and dependent on one another, Revelation and Theology are two different parallel systems that must not be blended together, for their laws of growth are as different as their natures. We have already seen that, like other sciences, Theology grows by continual readjustments and occasional reconstructions. Quite otherwise is the growth of Revelation, which in some sense is not a growth at all, but an unfolding of what was implied in the Revelation of Christ. The great master of some school of music or painting may well be surprised one day by a disciple who in turn may become the founder of a new school, the revealer of a fuller and higher spirit. But the greatest of the saints has but some share and measure of the plenitude of Christ's spirit. Collectively they stand to

Him as does a prism to the white light of the sun, breaking up and revealing the inexhaustible riches of His simple perfection. And so, too, the love-inspired language and action in which they have revealed their inward experience of things divine stand to His master-revelation as so much comment and illustration; as partial revelations of the same spirit, but in no wise possibly adding to its substance. With it, as controlling rule and criterion, they make up a growing body of revelation whose parts are not connected dialectically like those of theology, but are related to one another as all the works of the same school of art, namely, as various manifestations of one and the same master-spirit. And in this living, growing body of variously inspired utterances—in which the spirit-life of Christ and the Church spontaneously clothes and reveals itself, we have the subject-matter of theological reflection. This is that world of spiritual experience which it seeks to name and understand, ever readjusting, and at times reconstructing, itself according as the treasures of Christ's revelation, unearthed in ever greater abundance by the spiritual labour of His saints, create a demand for wider and worthier conceptions. We may and must demand restatements of Theology, but to demand restatements of Revelation would be to confound it with Theology. We do not ask that Da Vinci's "Last Supper" should be corrected in the light of criticism; nor do we respect the Temperance proposal to substitute water for wine in our Eucharists. Inspired language is never "out of date," but shares the timelessness of the spirit. God will always be "our

Father in heaven," Christ will always be the Son, the Word of God, the Good Shepherd, the Lamb of God, the Vine, the Light of the World, the Bread of Heaven.

7

Thus Revelation and Theology co-operate in the naming of God, in the formation of progressively worthier ideas and utterances about Him. Mere reflection and reasoning exercised on unchanging data degenerate into a barren, abstract scholasticism. The heart and spirit of Christ must supply fresh stores of experience for the theological mind to work upon if it is not to prey on its own vitals and weave mere cobwebs of the brain.

Perforce men must use their minds on Revelation as on all other experience; they must name, classify, and arrange it in their understanding for future use in the service of life. And since this may be done in two ways, rightly or wrongly, we need a science to ensure that it shall be done rightly. To repudiate all theology could not stop theological reflection, but would let it run riot into all manner of absurdities and superstitions. Could we possibly stop such reflection altogether, the streams of religious experience would at first run to waste, and eventually be dried up completely. When we read or listen to the fervid flow of inspired language, so careless of theological thought, so often professedly intolerant of it, we are too apt to forget how largely that inspiration has itself been fed and formed by an unconsciously imbibed theology.

Much insistence has been laid sometimes on the

entirely non-theological, or even anti-theological character of our Lord's teaching as set before us in the Synoptic Gospels. Not merely does He never address Himself to the intellect or insist on correct mental conceptions of divine things; not merely does He disdain the wise and prudent with their scholastic disputations and address Himself to babes in that inspired language of Revelation through which heart speaks to heart; but the very cause for which He sacrificed Himself in the interest of Truth was His steady warfare against a theology that had made vain the Word of God through the traditions of men. If this reading of the Gospels be right, if theology be something quite repugnant to the spirit of Christ, it is certainly somewhat perplexing to find so much theology, not merely in the later Gospel of St. John, but in the earliest documents of the New Testament, namely, in the writings of St. Paul. Is it likely, we may ask, that Christianity was so speedily corrupted into its direct opposite? And since not (for *nemo fit repente turpissimus*), must it not be a hasty inference that interprets Christ's opposition to a particular theology as a condemnation of all theology whatsoever?

He did not, however, combat theology with theology—the false with the true. Things had gone too far for any mere readjustment of a system that had long hardened itself out of all plasticity and power of accommodating itself to religious experience; that regarded the prophetic spirit as its natural enemy; that had become a yoke and a burden to souls instead of a support and deliverance. As it could no longer bend or adjust itself, it needed to be broken up and reconstituted by the power of that Spirit "which spake by the prophets." It was with the might of a vaster love, a vaster spirit, that Christ assailed this system, and tore through its bonds as Samson through the withes of Delilah. He had but to reveal the Father, the Divine Reality, as it lived and wrought in His own spirit, in order to show up the paltriness and unworthiness of that presentment which loveless intellectual pedantry had made of God, His will and His way. His mission and method were prophetic, not theological. In due relation, as we have seen, Prophecy and Theology are allies; but when either encroaches on the other's rights and liberties they become enemies for the time being. But the enmity cannot be permanent. As prophecy presupposes theology in its very inspiration and aim, so it requires it for the garnering of its fruits. If Christianity was the creation of prophecy and not of theology, yet without theology of some sort it could not have lived and fructified. If our Lord's zeal for the hallowing of His Father's Name took the form of righteous indignation against an unworthy theology whose presentment of God He refuted by confronting it with the Realty as living in His own spirit; if He was content to shatter the false system without Himself reconstructing a truer—this was only because Revelation was the first and most pressing need, and because theological reflection could be better deferred till the creative period was passed and its results might be arranged and set in order at leisure.

8

And what sort of presentment of God was that which our Saviour confronted with the living Reality—with the Father as revealed in the Son—and which He shattered to pieces as a libel on the Name of the Father?

In judging the Rabbis and Pharisees we need great discrimination, lest we mistake the spirit of the dominant clique of a passing day for the abiding spirit of the Jewish people and its rulers. From the New Testament and the early Christian documents we only know of that school and tendency of Judaism with which Christianity came into direct collision. We hear so exclusively of the points of difference that we easily forget the vast area of agreement. Not only was the earliest Christian Church made up of Jews almost entirely, but such a movement within the bosom of Judaism would not have been possible had the spirit of (what we may conveniently, if not quite justly call) Pharisaism held so universal and undisputed a sway as commonly supposed. The fields were already ripe unto the harvest when Christ thrust in His sickle. There were many sheep in Israel, His own already, who would recognize His voice as that of the Spirit "which spake by the prophets." Even amongst the "teachers in Israel" Nicodemus represented a class or party, and among the scribes and law-doctors there were many "not far from the Kingdom of God." All this vague and diffused Christianity was drawn into Christ, as a nebula into the sun, and in

Him became definite, active, and vocal. What others guessed, He knew and touched; what they groped after, He possessed and comprehended.

With this proviso we can talk freely of Pharisaism as the dead element of Judaism with which He was at war just because it was strangling the living element. After all, it was only a particular manifestation of a disease to which every institutional religion is liable, and as such it is an ever-recurrent phenomenon.

Since man mirrors God in his own heart, he necessarily tends to represent Him in his own image and likeness. The soul of superstition and idolatry is not mental error, but moral corruption: a pure heart is the eye which sees God straight even through the crookedest theology, as a corrupt heart sees Him crooked even through the straightest. The God of Pharisaism was therefore simply a deified Pharisee, and as such could not command the reverence and love of mankind.

Conscious of sitting in the chair of Moses, of being God's official representatives on earth, the scribes and Pharisees would have needed unusual elevation of character had they not been continually tempted to cover their own ideas and prepossessions with the mantle of divine authority, and to say, "Thus saith the Lord" far more freely and readily than was warranted. Even those who might have scrupled so to canonize their personal views and judgments would have had little scruple when the interest of their caste and its tradition were at stake, loyalty to which may have honestly seemed to them identical with loyalty to God and conscience. Yet egotism is not less but more dangerous when it is the egotism of corporation, for which no one member is singly responsible.

When authority is conceived as a licence to make things true or false, good or evil, at will, rather than as involving a duty of finding out and declaring what is true and right, its exercise can only bring God down towards man's level instead of raising man up towards God's. Those who call themselves His representatives on earth may, if unscrupulous, end by treating Him as their representative in heaven, bound to ratify all their wishes and further all their designs. Thus the will of the scribes and Pharisees had been canonized as the Will of God, their notions and ideas were the Truth of God, what they fought for as His glory and honour was really their own. The spirit of their clique was put forward as His spirit. The narrow nationalism, the political aims and intrigues of the Pharisees, were His also. It was He who laid the law, a soul-destroying burden, on men's weak shoulders; who enslaved men to His Sabbaths; who spoke to them in technicalities that wearied their brains and left their hearts cold. And even when God revealed Himself, as He always does, to the hearts of His children, they dare not trust what their hearts told them of His fatherly goodness, for they were ever confronted by this official presentment of His Will and Character, by this Pharisee-God, to which in some sense their allegiance was due. Thus the official teaching which should have fostered their spiritual growth cramped and obstructed it;

and this, not because it was official, or because it was a theology and a tradition, but because it was a dead theology sterilized in political or non-religious interests, in the interests of authority viewed as an end in itself and not as a means; in the interests of the rulers rather than of the ruled; of the teachers rather than of the taught; and all this because it refused to be continually fed and re-shaped by religious experience, and turned a deaf ear to Prophecy and Revelation.

Hence it resulted that the Name of God was brought into dishonour, and fell as a harsh discord on the spiritual ear, so that His very children were alienated from Him by those who should have gathered them in confidence to His feet.

Our Lord's anger was not therefore against theology or science, but against that egotism and corruption of heart which is as hostile to true knowledge as it is to true religion, "Woe unto you lawyers, for you have taken away the key of knowledge: ye entered not in yourselves, and them that were entering in ye hindered."

9

The desire for the hallowing of God's Name is a desire that He may be so rightly known as to be rightly reverenced and loved as our Father in heaven. It looks to that knowledge which is to be read from the book of life and love; which is continually fed by experience and directed to ampler experience. It is a desire kindled by the contrast between what is and what ought to be; between God libelled and dishonoured, and God as He ought to be known, loved, and reverenced. And fuel is heaped on the flame by the thought of all the lies that have been spoken in the name of God's Truth, and of all the wickedness that has been wrought in the name of God's Will; and not only by this direct dishonouring of His Name, but by the indirect dishonour which accrues to the father through those who bear the name of son only to disgrace it.

Plainly it is not to be a barren desire that burns itself away fruitlessly. The heat must be turned to work, and fed by the fuel of prayer only for the sake of work. God not only prays in us, but works in us; the prayer is but the beginning of the work. It but fosters the germinating seed still hidden in the bosom of the earth.

V

THE SECOND PETITION

Adveniat Regnum Tuum.—Thy Kingdom come

I

It is not too much to say that this is the central and governing petition of the whole prayer, which is the prayer of the Kingdom. The hallowing of God's Name is but subordinate as a means to the coming of His Kingdom; the doing of His Will is but the effect and consequence of it. The petitions that remain are entirely governed by, and directed to, those that precede.

This, then, is the dominant desire of Christ's heart,

the dominant vision of His mind, the dominant aim of His will and endeavour. We might look on it as the briefest and most essential definition of His spirit. It is not therefore surprising that much controversy has been raised as to what our Lord meant by the Kingdom of Heaven or the Kingdom of God; whether He understood it as internal or external, or both; whether by the external Kingdom He meant the Catholic Church militant on earth, or a millennium, or the Church finally triumphant in heaven. With these controversies we deal but indirectly according to our method, which is, to ask ourselves first what the terms meant for His hearers, Peter, Andrew, and the rest, and then what they should mean for us. In other words, we are studying, not a prayer which our Lord prayed, but one which He taught us to pray. In the difference between the cruder and more childish sense which the petition would have borne for the least sympathetic of His hearers, and the deeper and fuller sense it has come to bear for the Christian consciousness, we have a revelation of Christ's spirit. We see it patiently and sweetly struggling with the earthliness of man's thoughts and affections, and raising them gradually but surely to the spiritual level. And in the study of this process we find perhaps our best hope of entering into the mind of the Christ on earth. The later developments of the idea of the Kingdom in the mind of His saints furnish the best clue to His spirit, "of whose fulness they have all received," and of which each manifests some particular aspect.

2

According to the popular conception of Christ's immediate hearers, the Kingdom of God, or of Heaven, meant the triumph of Israel, God's peculiar people; not the triumph merely of a nation, but of a church, a theocracy; of a nation which was God's representative on earth, with which His Name and His cause were identified : " Not unto us, O God, but to Thy Name give the glory."

The national and the religious interests were then in some sort united. Where the sentiment of nationalism was stronger than that of religion, the divine interests were interpreted and measured by the national. Where, as in the prophets, the religious sentiment dominated, the national interests were interpreted and measured by the divine. In the former case God was brought down to man's level; in the latter, man raised to God's. There, the notion of the Heavenly Kingdom was materialized; here, it was spiritualized. The ebb and flow of religious fervour, alternating periods of depression and revival, of backsliding and repentance, had not however been inconsistent with a slow progress from less to more worthy conceptions, and had made it fairly clear that the identification of God with Israel was conditional and not absolute; that God might for a time, though surely not for ever, cast off His people for their sins and infidelities. Israel, it was recognized, could not triumph till he was holy even as his God was holy. His holiness was the essential condition of his triumph ; but that it was the substance of his triumph was the secret of only a few. For most, the national glory was the reward; righteousness was but the condition; the Kingdom was on the same plane as that of David and Solomon, only that God Himself should reign vicariously in the Messias, His Son, a righteous King over a righteous Israel, and that in Him all the subjugated nations of the earth should be blessed. This was the Kingdom of Heaven, the Rule of God upon earth.

But, moreover, it was to be a Kingdom *from* heaven, a new Jerusalem descending from above. For after many tribulations and backslidings Israel had learned to despair of his own strength. As little as he could deliver himself from his oppressors, so little could he attain that righteousness which would compel God to his aid. His hope was only in God's mercy, in His fidelity to His promises to Abraham, Isaac, and Jacob. If he but cried out to Him, if he but struggled to purify himself and to meet Him, God would surely, in the person of His Messias, burst through the heavens and come down to cleanse and justify him and to establish his throne on the basis of righteousness.

This was the hope and prayer of the religious Pharisees at the time of our Lord. To hasten this event by penance and purification as they understood then, i.e. by a rigorous fidelity to every letter of God's law, was their noble endeavour. Formerly the deliverance had been conceived more in the national interest and less in the religious. It was to be a triumph of Israel indiscriminately, and the confusion of the Gentiles. But now we find the germ of

S. Paul's distinction between Israel after the flesh and Israel after the spirit. It is only the righteous Israelite that shall sit down to meat in the Kingdom with Abraham, Isaac, and Jacob. The saints and prophets of old shall rise from their tombs and together with living saints shall be caught up to meet the Messias as He comes in the clouds, and shall sit as His assessors to judge the world. Thus the event took the character of a Day of Judgment, a separation of sheep from goats, a winnowing of grain from chaff. Hence the call to repentance, to preparation, that as many as possible might make themselves worthy to enter into the Kingdom of God.

In this conception of the Kingdom we have the result of a gradual entering into the deeper sense of Old Testament prophecy; of a discerning between the letter and the spirit; between the symbolism and the divine mystery. Even to the prophets themselves the distinction may not always have been clear. For them it may have hardly been possible to dissociate that triumph of God and His cause, of which their glowing faith assured them, from the triumph of Israel after the flesh, His chosen people, His earthly representative. That same Israel, purified and glorified, was their highest expression of the Reign of Righteousness; and for them this expression may have contained but little conscious symbolism. Still, even such a Golden Age had to be presented in terms of one that was brass or iron; and to the carnal-minded it was necessary to express spiritual prosperity and glory under the figure of temporal.

Such figures taken literally had given birth to grosser and more popular conceptions of the Messianic Kingdom founded on the misreading of prophecy. Then, as now, it was only the steady working of the prophetic spirit itself, whether through the agency of acknowledged prophets, or through that of the religious-minded section of the community, that resisted this materializing tendency and effected even such a refinement of the Messianic idea as the Pharisees had attained to in our Lord's time.

We say commonly that the wish is father to the thought; that our hopes shape our beliefs. The stronger a man's desire to see the Kingdom of God upon earth, the more will he be disposed to believe in the proximate realization of that desire. This is true of all idealists at all times. Faith in God means faith that what ought to be will be; and this faith is never deceived. But in our judgment as to what ought to be and as to what God wills, we may easily be deceived. It is certain that "truth is great and will prevail"; here we are not deceived; but when we identify truth with some cherished belief of our own, and expect this to prevail, we often expose our faith to shipwreck. Similarly, a prophet or idealist may err in his judgment as to the manner and time of God's deliverance. He is one to whom the barrier that divides the temporal and eternal, the actual and the ideal, the present and the future, have become more or less transparent; whose sense of perspective is gone; whose spirit is in conscious touch with those deepest roots and springs of reality which determine the course of history. But the judgment as to what ought to be always has reference to certain facts already in existence. Unless we know exactly what is, we cannot say exactly what ought to be. The prophet, as one in keen sympathy with the Divine Spirit, will feel at once what ought to be, *given* that his knowledge of what is, is adequate. This, however, it can never be altogether. Hence his forecasts have always an element of hypothesis. He is prone to narrow the stage of the divine drama and to hasten its conclusion ; to conceive the Kingdom as at once too narrow and too near.

Thus at every period of religious revival, when men are longing and looking for the Kingdom of God, they are ready to be persuaded, and to persuade themselves, that it is near, even at the very gates ; to translate the inward event into an outward one.

Such a public conviction of the nearness of the Kingdom had obtained in Israel at the time when John the Baptist came with his call to repentance and preparation. He was not merely, like the other prophets, a preacher of the Kingdom, but more especially of its nearness : " Repent, for the Kingdom of Heaven *is at hand.*" It was this nearness that stirred men to repentance and sent them flocking to the Jordan, as many a time since the expectation of a general catastrophe, or of the end of the world, has roused men to realize the nothingness of all but eternal interests. Hurtful as such erroneous expectations have sometimes been to social order and progress, not only as fostering a certain lawlessness in the irreligious, but as leading the religious to neglect a world which they believe doomed to such speedy destruction, yet the call from dreams of time to the realities of eternity has usually been an abiding gain for humanity far outweighing such temporal loss. Though not in the literal sense of the Baptist's hearers, the Kingdom of Heaven was indeed near; time was short, eternity was long, repentance was urgent. As the Kingdom itself was a more spiritual Kingdom than men deemed, so also was its nearness a more spiritual nearness. What is spiritual is not less real, but far more so. It was nearer than they could ever understand; even at the very doors.

3

We have, then, a fairly accurate idea of what the Kingdom of God will have meant for those who listened to our Lord. That notion of theirs was the rough material which He had to shape into a less inadequate expression of His own spirit, adding, taking away, refining, transfiguring.

All prophecy dealt with the Kingdom of God, with that Ideal ever struggling to birth in the womb of the Actual. The Baptist proclaimed its nearness. Christ proclaimed its presence. In Him it had come; in Him God's Will was already done on earth as it is in heaven; in Him the Ideal had become actual, the Word was made flesh, and dwelt in our midst. "The Kingdom of Heaven is in your midst." Whatever these words mean, it is hard to suppose that they simply assert the internal character of God's Kingdom. They do not enunciate a principle, but a fact—the fact that the Kingdom has come. Could it be said to have come into the hearts of a miscellaneous crowd? Is it not rather that "there stood in the midst of them one whom they knew not," one in whom the realization of the Kingdom had already begun on earth? *L'État c'est moi:* He was the King, and He was the Kingdom. Grow how it will, as a vine stretching its branches all over the world, the Church is nothing but Christ. The saints but partake of His fulness. They but manifest what was latent in His spirit. The fulness was there when He was there; the end was involved in the beginning; the fruit in the germ.

After the fulness, there can be no new revelation; only an endless unfolding. It is only in this sense, and in reference to this unfolding, that the Christian can pray: "Thy Kingdom come"—not in the sense of the prophets of old, who vainly desired to see what we see and to hear what we hear.

In substance, therefore, the Kingdom had already come; what had yet to come was its plenary manifestation. The seed was sown, the least of the seeds evading observation. Noiselessly, when men were asleep, the world had slid past the winter solstice of its history and the era of a new life had begun.

4

Never do we find our Lord directly discussing or controverting the Messianic ideas prevailing around Him. As the expression of the highest religious hopes of His people, they were sacred for Him, and to be handled with all reverence; nor would He with a ruthless criticism hastily shatter what was, for so many of His little ones, the consecrated and the only possible vehicle of eternal truths. He knew that no embodiment avails for the religious spirit but that which it spontaneously fashions for itself; that it was futile to work directly on the embodiment, or otherwise than by enlightening and purifying the spirit. Hence His attitude towards the material and visible side of the popular Messianic hopes was largely one of indifference: "The flesh profiteth nothing." His whole insistence was on the religious values and significations: "It is the Spirit that quickeneth." He treats the materialistic bias of the general mind with tenderness, or at worst with a kindly irony, as one who thoroughly understands and tolerates as inevitable a narrower outlook than his own. The unique and perfect purity of His heart went with a perfect spirituality of conception unattainable for others. It was through the purification of their hearts that He sought to spiritualize their ideas and slowly detach them from a vision and conception shaped by their desires. We find Him therefore not discussing the form of their beliefs, but pressing their spiritual significance and consequences. If at times He adopts the current literalism, we feel that He is speaking in parables and mysteries; that under the old sounds He is insinuating a deeper sense, intelligible only to the few that have ears to hear; that He speaks as a father would speak to his little children, preoccupied about matters whose truth is not even worth discussing, heedless as to the deeper sense of the tale that they hear, and only anxious to know if it be true. What were living interests for the popular religious imagination were dead for Him; and conversely. "How shall the dead rise? with what bodies shall they come?"—there is the popular interest. "He that believeth in Me, though he were dead, yet shall he live; and he that liveth and believeth shall never die"—there is our Lord's interest. In many matters the affirmations of the Pharisees and the negations of the Sadducees were to Him equally irrelevant, equally vitiated by a misplacement of the true centre of interest. Of the two, His sympathies will have been more with the zeal of narrow-minded fanatics than with an easy tolerance begotten of worldliness and indifference to religion, or than with a certain sort of hostility to externalities that renders as excessive a homage to their importance as does the most rigorous defence of them.

We may then be sure that those features of the current Messianic hopes which appealed in any way to personal or national egotism, or which gratified the childish wonder-lust of popular imagination, or which were fabricated by the merely speculative curiosity of commentators and scribes, or whose interest was other than purely spiritual and religious, formed no substantial part of the Gospel of Christ. God and man; God in man; man in God—this was what it all meant for Him; this was the sole and sovereign end in the interest of which His spirit moulded and refined the rude stuff offered Him by popular beliefs.

5

To conclude from this that the Kingdom of God is something fully realized again and again in each individual soul which subjects itself perfectly to the dominion of divine love, that it is in no sense a general and external event, would be not only a false, but an entirely uncritical perversion of our Lord's meaning. He came not to destroy, but to fulfil; not to break off, but to carry on, the prophetic process which had shaped the current Messianic hopes; not to narrow, but to broaden their import, to give them ever a more world-wide, universal, eternal significance. To have interpreted them as no more than a parable of each man's spiritual life would have been to explain them away, to treat them as the dreamings of national vanity. It would not have been to develop and transcend the current doctrine of the Kingdom, but to deny it altogether; or to accept it only in an entirely equivocal sense. As the history of an organism reproduces itself analogously and with variations, in each of its parts and members, so, it is true, the history of the Church, of the Kingdom of God, is enacted in small in each several soul, which in its own way is also a spouse of Christ, a Kingdom of God. But it is so in a secondary and dependent sense; the primary sense is social, collective, universal. We may lawfully apply the petition, "Thy Kingdom come," to our own personal sanctification; but that is not what the petition directly meant, or was intended to mean, for those to whom it was taught by our Lord. He meant what all around Him meant by the Kingdom of God; but what they viewed through the distorting medium of imperfectly purified affections He beheld through the flawless crystal of a perfect heart. It was the same foreseen event for them and for Him; the difference was one of clouded vision and clear. That event was nothing more nor less than the consummation of the long process of human history: nay, of the secular conflict between good and evil, light and darkness, in the triumph of God's cause. But what the prophets had seen in part, and through a glass darkly, He who was in the bosom of the Father, and of the fulness of whose spirit they had but received a measure, saw face to face. In His perfect love the perfect truth of the matter was implied and felt—for it was a love that could not be content with the narrower and less spiritual conception of the Kingdom, but broadened and purified it to suit its own imperative demand. And it could demand no less than the breaking down of all barriers between God and man, between man and man; no less than the gathering of the whole spirit-world into one communion round the feet of the "Father of spirits"; no less than the final fusion of many discordant minds, hearts, and wills into one divine harmony of truth, love, and aim.

Here is the essence of the matter. The circumstances under which this Kingdom is to be realized are comparatively irrelevant. That is what Divine Charity, what the spirit of Christ implies, postulates, reveals. Nor does this social conception of the Kingdom conflict with the truth that in the sole person of Christ it was already realized; that in Him it had come down upon earth from heaven. For He was the Kingdom only in so far as the spiritual Church and her children were latent in Him as Eve and the whole human race were in Adam.

So far as the current Messianic hopes of His time looked dimly towards such a consummation of human history, they were echoed and re-echoed by His heart. So far as they looked to anything else they were dead for Him.

Of His own place and function in that spiritual Kingdom—as the true or heavenly Messias; as the King of the catholic, world-wide, spiritual Israel; as the term of the world's best aspirations; as the source of its best inspirations—He has spoken in no obscure language. Through Him and with Him as the head of the mystic organism we have access to, and union with, the Father; "No man cometh to the Father but by Me."

Against the individualistic conception of the Kingdom as consisting primarily in the subjection of the soul to God, and in the peaceful ordering of her several faculties, ideas, and affections under His rule, we must notice that for each single member the spiritual organism to which it belongs is something relatively external, a world to which it has to adjust itself, in which and through which it lives; a Kingdom whose rule it obeys, whose ends it serves. Life implies environment. The Communion of Saints is the environment of each several saint; it is the kingdom into which he desires to enter—the Kingdom of

Heaven. When he prays for its advent, he is not praying directly for himself or for his own spiritual perfection, but for something outside and above himself; for it is God's Spirit that prays in him for a divine and universal end. Thus the religious Jew who, like Simeon, looked and longed for the consolation of Israel, for the triumph of God's cause as he conceived it, was not far from the Kingdom of God. For he sought it in an event of world-wide and eternal import; in an end that took him out of his narrower self and raised him to the spiritual plane of disinterested goodness. In so doing it also sanctified him individually. For sanctity consists precisely in such an elevation to a sharing of the divine outlook and the Divine Will; in the dying to self and the living to God.

6

If this communion or society of the saints with one another in God, and through Christ, is the Kingdom of Heaven in the deepest and most essential acceptation of the term, yet that term is also used in derived and dependent senses of the sanctified soul, or of the visible Church, or generally of the realization of God's Will upon earth.

The question of the circumstances, the where and when of the final triumph of truth and righteousness, is undoubtedly a subordinate one, neither affecting our faith in that triumph nor materially altering our duties of conflict and labour in the cause of God upon earth. It was upon earth that the Jews looked for the establishment of the eternal Kingdom. The

Kingdom of Satan which it was to supplant was upon earth. In our Lord the Kingdom had (in substance) come down from heaven upon earth. The disciples were to pray: "Thy Will be done on earth, as it is in heaven"—words explicative of the preceding petition, "Thy Kingdom come." The Millennium heresy blindly adhered to the letter of this doctrine. But the Church, taught and guided by the spirit of Christ, soon distinguished its kernel from its husk and recognized that this earth could never be transformed into heaven; that the eternal Kingdom of God belonged to eternity and not to time; that flesh and blood could not inherit it. Unattainable, however, as might be the ideal of a world like ours, peopled by saints alone and ruled solely by the Will of God, yet, as contrasted with the narrower Jewish conception, this notion of a spiritual and universal Israel upon earth served both as a figure or embodiment of the other-world Kingdom, and as the unreachable goal of those prayers and endeavours by which it was to be realized.

In speaking of "Practicality" and of the danger of "works without faith," we insisted on the distinction between the spiritual, immanent side of action, and its external fruit or effect. The former as belonging to the spirit-life and to the inner world is of sovereign importance; the latter possesses but a dependent and conditional importance as the object, end, and occasion of the former. The aim, as an event of the eternal order, is more important than its attainment, which is an event of the temporal order; the will to feed the hungry is a greater good than the bodily satisfaction to which it is directed. So, too, the endeavour to realize God's Kingdom perfectly in the visible order, though doomed to failure, is the necessary condition and the unfailing cause of its realization in the spiritual order. No will can be united to God's and built into the Communion of Saints that is not firmly set upon the overthrow of evil and the triumph of good through the length and breadth of the earth. Hence we have to do with two interpenetrating worlds—one spiritual and eternal, the other visible and transitory. In each the Kingdom of God has to be established: there, in its very essence or substance; here, in its signs and manifestations.

There we have the invisible or spiritual Church on earth, the secret communion of all those whose wills are knit through Christ with God's, and who form but part of that vaster communion which embraces those saints who have passed out of the limits of time and place. For the spiritual heaven is in process of formation, and is fed through roots that are netted in the soil of sinful earth, where day by day new souls are fashioned for their place and function in its organism. Thus heaven, though transcendent with respect to earth, is also immanent. If it stretches infinitely beyond it, yet it also permeates and passes through it, and draws substance from it for its own life and development.

But, on the side of its visible manifestation, God's Kingdom on earth stands for something that is at once the effect and the condition of the invisible Church; something that, roughly speaking, is its embodiment. It stands for the sum-total of those external conditions of the spiritual life which should be the aim of religion in its own interest, and of which it is said, "Seek ye first the Kingdom of God and His righteousness, and *all these things* shall be added unto you," and, "Your Heavenly Father knoweth that ye have need of these things." Temporal things, thus ordered in the interests of eternal, do themselves constitute the Kingdom of God in a secondary and dependent sense; they make an environment in which the inner life can reach its highest and widest development. The term of such an amelioration of present conditions may be unthinkable and unattainable as an ideal, but we have no doubt about the "direction" which the process should take. The Jewish conception of the Messianic reign on earth erred not only by its poverty and narrowness, but by its finality. It made righteousness the condition rather than the substance of God's triumph, which substance it sought in an absolute and final amelioration of society. For our Lord the reign of righteousness, the spiritual and invisible Kingdom, was the great end; social amelioration but its instrument and condition; final and absolute amelioration but the ever-receding horizon of our progress. Paradox though it be, while a "golden age" on earth is the goal and stimulus of all moral and spiritual endeavour, yet its attainment would be fatal to morality and religion. The truth is, we are to work for ever towards it, certain that we shall never overtake it; that tasks accomplished will ever breed more tasks; that every attainment makes higher and wider attainments possible and necessary.

7

In Christ the Kingdom of God, both spiritual and visible, descended on earth. In Him the twofold process began. For out of Him, too, has grown the visible Christian Church and Christian civilization in the service of the spiritual Church or Kingdom.

When we speak of the spiritual Church as a kingdom, we are using a similitude rather than a metaphor, and may not press the correspondence point for point. In some respects, but not in all, it is like a kingdom. The very first idea of kingship, especially in ancient times, was that of dominion and authority, which implies a power of moral, and eventually of physical, coercion. But in the spiritual Kingdom the service is free or it is nothing; it must be the service of sons, not of slaves; of love, not of fear. The Heavenly King is also the Heavenly Father. His Fatherhood is the root of His Kingship. The spirit cannot be forced; it can only be drawn or allured. No command, under whatever penalty or bribe, can make us see what we do not see, feel what we do not feel, will what we do not will. God is the sovereign rule of right thought and love and will; but He works from within, shaping the spirit in accordance with its own laws. An authority in matters of truth or of taste means a standard that is set before us to waken our interest and provoke our activity. Such is the authority of Christ, the King of the spiritual Kingdom. He went before us as our Shepherd to draw us after Him; He showed us an example, that we might freely follow it; He did not dominate or command, as the rulers of the nations, but was in our midst as one who serves and helps. And in all this He but represented and revealed the Father. This, then, is the meaning of authority or Kingship in the spiritual order. And under Christ in this Heavenly Kingdom there is a hierarchy of lesser authorities, of those saints who with Him shall judge the world even as He judges it —even as light judges darkness—who partake in varying measures of His fulness, grace for grace, and draw us by example, step by step, upwards to His throne, according to our several needs and capacities; who cluster round Him each in his own orbit as planets round the sun, reflecting His glory and making with Him one system or spiritual universe. If Christ lives for us in the written Gospels and in the preaching of the Church, yet He lives for us far more in those who are filled with His spirit, and whose example silently sways us and brings us under His dominion. Of these spiritual authorities it can be said in no equivocal sense, " He that heareth you heareth Me; and he that despiseth you despiseth Me and Him that sent Me." Or again: " As the living Father hath sent Me, so send I you." To them the Light of the World has said, " Ye are the light of the world"; and the Redeemer has said, " Ye are the salt of the earth" ; and the Good Shepherd has said," Feed My lambs; feed My sheep." In the measure that His spirit lives and speaks in them, what they bind on earth is bound in heaven; what they loose on earth is loosed in heaven; whose sins they forgive are forgiven, and whose sins they retain are retained.

For their mind is His mind, their judgment His judgment, their will His will. Thus the features of the hierarchic and visible Church are repeated analogously and spiritually in the invisible Church to which it is ministerial as the body is to the soul.

True it is that the members on earth of this Communion of Saints are visible to our bodily eyes; yet their membership in that society is a secret known to God alone with certainty, however brightly their light may shine before men and proclaim them children of the Father in heaven. Moreover, the bond that binds them together and gives each his place and function in the mystic organism of Christ's body, as a separate and special manifestation of one and the same spirit, is a bond visible only in the light of eternity. Scattered through the ages and nations there is no outward social tie between them; only the inward tie of unity of spirit, unity of aim, unity of faith: "The Lord knoweth those that are His," and He alone. Their worship is that inward worship in spirit and in truth of which all outward worship is but the expression, and without which it is dead; it is the worship of the spirit that loves God alone and above all, that subjects itself unreservedly to the Sovereign Truth and Love and Goodness; it is the practical worship and sacrifice of Him who was obedient unto death, even the death of the Cross. And though it is not a public worship, yet it is a social and collective worship in virtue of the mystical union which binds Christ and His members in one body through one spirit, and makes their sacrifices together with His into one age-long, world-wide, pure sacrifice offered for the world's redemption from the rising of the sun to the going down of the same.

8

This spiritual Kingdom of God is what lies behind the visible Kingdom, and lends it all its desirableness as an object of prayer and endeavour. The visible is sought for the sake of the spiritual. Yet the two are not explicitly distinguished, but are taken together as a whole in the petition : " Thy Kingdom come."

The visible, external Kingdom is best described as a foreshortened statical presentment of that endless process of amelioration of social conditions in the interests of the spirit which was inaugurated, on a new level, by the advent of Christ. It represents, symbolically, the final result of a task which can have no end; fixing the direction, rather than marking the goal, of a race that knows no rest. For " here we have no abiding city," though we must be for ever building. With Christ this external Kingdom had come in substance; with every new stage of Christian civilization it has come in greater fulness ; and yet its perfect accomplishment remains an ever-receding goal.

We need not delay to dwell on the obvious relation of mutual dependence between civilization and Christianity, founded on the indissoluble unity of man's spirit-life; or to dissipate the superficial illusion that the Christian as such can be indifferent to all but the explicitly religious interests of human life; that he can look on questions of art, science, sociology, and politics as unconnected with the Kingdom of God and His righteousness. Not one of these members of life's organism can suffer or prosper, but religion and all the rest suffer or prosper with it. It is true that Christ did not come with any direct doctrine about art or science, or economics or politics; nor did He commission or authorize His Apostles to reform civilization in these respects. All their efforts were to be directed solely to the religious life of the spirit, to the adjustment of its immediate relations to God and man; they were to concentrate on the ultimate roots and springs of the spirit-life, on the sovereign interest and end of all. But we must not confound the special vocation of the apostle, priest, or prophet with that of the Christian as such, or forget that the roots of life are cultivated for the sake of the fruits. The Christian as such, and as distinct from the minister of religion, must, according to his vocation and state of life, seek the Kingdom of God in every department of civilization, as the minister of religion seeks it in the soul of the Christian.

On the other hand, we must remember that specialization and co-ordination are the conditions of Christian civilization, as of every other sort of life; that the organism of human interests demands that religion, the supreme interest, should be committed to the care of a special institution with a ministry of its own, to the visible Church. As the deepest interest, religion influences the rest in the direct line, and not merely collaterally as the rest influence one another. It holds the position of head in the organism. Still, the head is not the body; and the members have independent, though subordinate rights of their own; and health demands that each part, the head included, shall have full right to develop itself in its own order and shall abstain from all encroachment on the rights of its fellow-members. Religion is the supreme, but it is not the sole, interest of life. If it would starve the others, it would soon perish itself. Hence the law of specialization requires that there should be a Church as well as schools, societies, and governments; and that by the harmonious working of these institutions the cause of God's visible Kingdom on earth should be furthered.

And this exigency our Lord Himself acknowledged when He first chose out the Apostles from the crowd of his disciples and sent them forth on the special task of ministering to the soul. And what His spirit then began it has subsequently carried on in the formation of the visible Church, with her outward government, her official ministry, her institutions, sacraments, doctrines. As an external institution this Church is more aptly (though with grave and profound differences) likened to a kingdom; for though its ultimate sanctions are spiritual and its strongest argument is, "If you love me, keep my commandments," yet no visible society can subsist without some measure of juridical authority exercised over those who choose to belong to it. Moreover, it is the net containing bad fish as well as good, the field abounding in tares as well as wheat; and for such a society purely spiritual authority is as insufficient as it would be for civil society. Still, its juridical coercion is not backed by physical force, but by the free choice by which its members subject themselves to its rule.

The function of this visible Church we have already described under its most general aspect, namely, that of bringing the leaven and the dough together in one vessel; of mediating, through its teachings and institutions, between saints and sinners, heaven and earth; between the spiritually rich and enlightened and the spiritually poor and ignorant; between the religiously active souls and the religiously passive souls, receiving from the former, breaking and distributing to the latter.

9

Though we must pray and work towards a state of things in which the visible Church and the spiritual Church on earth should be coincident and literally catholic and coextensive with the race, yet the coincidence and the catholicity must for ever remain directive ideals. Never in the present order of things will all the members of the visible Church be spiritually living; never will all the spiritually living be members of the visible Church.

Thus, when we pray, "Thy Kingdom come," what we pray for principally and absolutely, though perhaps only implicitly, is the increase of the Communion of Saints. What we pray for explicitly, though subordinately and conditionally, is the furtherance of God's visible Kingdom on earth, the establishment of those social conditions which make for the increase of inward religion. Chief among those conditions is that divine institution, the creation of Christ's spirit, which exists explicitly for the defence of the religious interest, namely, the visible Church, the special organ and embodiment of the spiritual Church, the earthly representative, counterpart, and sacrament of the Communion of Saints.

VI

THE THIRD PETITION

Fiat Voluntas tua in cœlo et in terra.—Thy Will be done on earth, as it is in heaven.

I

The fact that St. Luke omits this petition implies that it is virtually contained in the preceding, of which it must be regarded as the amplification, or the closer definition. Obviously it secures a more spiritual and religious understanding of the Heavenly Kingdom, and suggests the distinction between the essential and the merely dependent elements of the conception.

The relation between the inward and the outward, the spiritual and the visible, aspects of God's Kingdom on earth is one of mutual dependence, of action and reaction. The amelioration of society is at once an end of and a means to religion, which itself is an end of and a means to social reformation. Yet this is consistent with the truth that the inward is principal and essential; the outward, dependent and secondary. The will is not without the deed; but the will, as an event of the spiritual and eternal order, is more important than the deed; and this, even should the deed be hindered by causes outside the will. The spiritual Kingdom of God answers to the will, the visible Kingdom to the deed. In His saints collectively the Will of God reproduces itself progressively on earth. Through and in them He wills and prays and works; in so far, namely, as they are raised above the psychic self-seeking level to the spiritual plane, and lend themselves to be instruments of the Divine and Eternal Will. In this sum-total of good desires, aspirations, intentions, hopes, fears, joys, sorrows, regrets, His Will (viewed subjectively as a willing; as a spiritual act or energizing) is made present on earth in a finite and broken manner as the sunlight is made present when reflected from the myriad ripples on a lake. In the mystical Christ the Divine Will is incarnate and tabernacles here among us. God's spiritual Kingdom comes on earth just in the measure that His Will reproduces and expresses itself more variously and extensively in the hearts of men. In good will, in the willing of good, God's Spirit finds its most perfect likeness and reproduction in the finite order, and the world which came forth from the Father returns to His bosom once more.

It is not, however, in unconsciously willing what God wills that the highest union with Him is realized; but in the consciousness that this aim and desire unite us with the Eternal Will and are the evidence and result of the possession of our spirit by the Divine Spirit, which uses us as free instruments of its own operation; in the consciousness that in willing what God wills, namely, His Kingdom on earth, we are ultimately willing God Himself, from whom every lesser end borrows its goodness; that the utmost realization of all our ideals could not content us apart from God, with whom and through whom alone they possess an absolute value and goodness. The merely ethical life is a monologue; the religious life is essentially a dialogue. Until the cause of goodness, justice, and truth reveals itself to us in the will of Another, we are alone in our struggle. He walks with us in the way, and our hearts burn within us, but our eyes are held, and we know Him not.

Thus, this willing, this spiritual act, which constitutes us sons of God and members of the mystical Kingdom, is not merely a willing of what God wills, but it is principally a willing of God. And it is He who by His Spirit works this will in us.

2

Most of those who listened to our Lord will have understood this third petition very simply; not untruly for practical purposes, but with little sense of its deeper import.

Their apprehension of religious truth was imaginative rather than spiritual. Heaven was God's dwelling-place above the sky—much as it is described for us in the symbolism of the Apocalypse, which for them was not symbolism but fact. For them, it was the archetype of the earthly Jerusalem, that "city of the Great King"; an ethereal structure of glory and light inaccessible, where nearly all the grossness of matter, of flesh and blood, was purged away, where mortality was indued with immortality, and corruption with incorruption. Here legions and hierarchies of ministering spirits stood beholding the face of the Father, "even as the eyes of servants look to the beck of their master," intent to know and do His pleasure; for this was their meat and drink, the bread of their eternal life. Here there was but one mind, one love, one Will—even the Father's.

This was the ideal, "the pattern shown to Moses in the mount" to which earth should be conformed. And between earth and heaven, between the actual and the ideal, was set Jacob's ladder with angels ascending and descending, bearing censers of prayers and vials of grace; ministering to the elect and helping the saints in their struggle with evil, to the end that God's Will might at last be done as perfectly on sinful earth as it is in heaven.

Here we have mystical truth expressed in terms of the imagination, the value of which terms is not merely "pragmatic," as that of a guide to conduct, but representative, by way of analogy, of eternal realities that lie beyond the grasp of clear intelligence.

For the measureless height of the heavens above the earth speaks to us of God's transcendence, of the distance that divides His nature from ours, His ways from our ways, His thoughts from our thoughts. The light and glory of the heavenly Jerusalem are eloquent of the antithesis between the spiritual darkness of the actual state of humanity and the goal of our prayers and endeavours—the Kingdom of God, the Communion of Saints. In the spectacle of the heavenly hierarchies, pervaded and moved, each in its own order or function, by one and the same Divine Will, and making collectively its perfect organ and vehicle of expression, we see that spiritual world which is struggling to reproduce itself here upon earth, as the life buried under the winter soil strives to push forth and clothe the world in the glory of spring. And in the conception of ministrant angels, ascending and descending in the service of this end, we see an effort of the religious consciousness to overcome a too exclusive emphasis of God's distance and otherness, and to bring Him near even to the very heart of man; we see a recognition of the divine immanence, of the interpenetration and continuity of earth and heaven; of time and eternity; such a recognition as that of the Psalmist, who sings: "Lord, Thou hast searched me and known me; Thou knowest my down-sitting and my uprising; Thou understandest my thoughts afar off. Whither shall I go from Thy Spirit? whither shall I flee from Thy presence? If I ascend up into heaven, Thou art there; if I go down to the depths, Thou art there"— words in which we feel the conflict between the imaginative and the mystical apprehension of the same truth.

And let us remember that, our minds being what they are, we can never altogether strip spiritual truth of its imaginative clothing so as to apprehend it nakedly; nor can we think or speak of reality except in terms of appearances. When we seem to have shelled the kernel of simpler forms of religious conception, we have but removed an outer husk to reveal an inner; we have but substituted a less material for a more material mode of expression. A narrow intolerance of ruder forms betrays a forgetfulness of this necessary limitation. The truth that lies behind the veil of words is the same, be the veil more or less transparent; and it may well be that it is often more vividly felt and loved when it is less clearly revealed and apprehended.

If Thought, Feeling, and Will, the components of the spirit-life, are correlative and inseparable; if the attempt to make any one of them supreme and independent issues in confusion, yet there is a certain order in their mutual dependence that allows us to consider the spirit-life as completing itself in the act of will. In this sense Augustine may say: "We are wills and nothing else," without falling into the excesses of "Voluntarism"—as the counter fallacy to "Intellectualism" is sometimes called. A blind Will, such as Schopenhauer speaks of, that involves no consciousness of what it makes for, and no feeling concerning it, is hardly distinguishable from a physical force, and does not deserve the name of Will. We mean by will that act in which the spirit tends with all its power, and as far as in it lies, to realize an end which it sees and desires. It is pre-eminently the act by which the spirit freely makes and shapes its own character. We are what we will. It is precisely as Will, as a Will (and therefore a Personality) other than our own, that God is made known to us in the phenomena of Conscience (moral, intellectual, and æsthetic), and it is this revelation that transforms the monologue of the merely ethical into the dialogue of the religious life. When we disregard the imperative claims of what Conscience tells us we "ought" to be, or do, or think, or feel, we are sensible not only of an offence against our higher and truer self-interests, but, if we consider more closely, of antagonism to a Will that forces those interests upon us. It is by resistance that the Not-self is made known to us, whether it be the outer world, or God, or our fellow-man. And it is by the subject-matter of that resistance that the nature or character of the Not-self is revealed, be it material or spiritual; be it lower, higher than, or equal to ourselves. The subject-matter of the conflict of Conscience is spiritual, eternal, absolute, universal. Such, therefore, is the character of the Not-self which there resists us. It is a spiritual, eternal, absolute Will other than our own.

It is not only difficult, but impossible for us to think of the relation between this Will and our own, except in terms of bodily things which can be counted and set over against one another, or united by contact or by mixture and fusion. If we talk of union or sameness with God, our thought becomes pantheistic; if of distinction and separateness, it becomes materialistic. So, as before, we shall pass by the metaphysical root of the matter, and speak only of its ethical manifestations in life and conduct; we shall speak of union with the Divine Will in the sense of willing the same things as God wills.

Plainly this union can never be perfect, since we can no more apprehend the absolute Good than the absolute Truth. But it is one thing to move in the right direction, at however great a distance from the goal; another, to move aside or in the opposite direction. Our heart can be "right" with God, and even perfectly right with God, though always with the possibility of indefinitely greater attainment. And this rectitude or conformity is the end of our whole moral struggle: "Thy Will be done on earth, as it is in heaven." We have to *make* ourselves will what God wills.

Since the true spiritual Self, potential in all of us, is the image and likeness of God, to find God, to be united with God, is morally the same thing as to find and be united with our true self. Only when He reigns over us do we truly reign over ourselves and attain full self-mastery, self-possession, self-determination.

Between the psychic individual will and the disinterested spiritual will in each of us there is a virtual relation of otherness and opposition, and a possibility of conflict or of agreement. The choice left to the freedom of the spirit is that of either subjecting the psychic life and interests to its own, or else of lending itself to the service of the psychic self and its desires. When it prays, "Father, not my will, but Thine," "my will" means the interests of the psychic separate self, of the spirit so far as, sometimes lawfully, sometimes unlawfully, it identifies itself with this individual organism which serves it; which it may duly care for, but may not serve. "Thy Will" means the spirit's own disinterested will viewed as identical with and imposed by the Divine

Will. "Not my will, but Thine," is the end of the whole process of the spirit's self-formation and self-reformation—the process by which it appropriates the Will of God and the Life of God; which Life, as freely proffered to its free acceptance, is the Grace of God: "The Grace of God is Eternal Life." God's Will is as natural and necessary a condition of the spirit-life as the rock is a condition of the limpet's life. It is by holding fast to God's Will that the spirit appropriates its subsistence, immobility, eternity.

We have seen in what sense it is true that the spirit reigns over, masters, determines itself only when God reigns over, masters, and determines it; that it is most free and independent when it is most subject and dependent. For that which is subjected, mastered, and determined is the psychic self, i.e. the spirit so far as it tends to identify itself unduly with its individual embodiment. That which rules and masters is the spiritual self, i.e. the spirit so far as, true to its own nature, it identifies itself with God. Freedom, self-determination, is what the spirit struggles for. When we say that Christ has delivered us and given us back to ourselves, we mean that He has delivered the spirit from servitude to the psychic self and has subjected its former tyrant to its service. It is of the psychic self that we ask obedience; we could no more ask it of the spiritual self than we could ask it of God; for the spiritual will is coincident with God's Will.

Personality, in the moral sense of the term, means spiritual freedom and self-mastery; and admits of endless measures of depth and extension. So far as we are passively borne along by our feelings, our habits and inclinations, so far as we are but wheels in the great mechanism of nature and are governed by physical, physiological, and psychological laws without attempting to use and control them, just so far are we things and not persons. We are persons in the measure that we oppose ourselves to all this mechanism, and through the understanding of it, are able to subject and use it to spiritual ends.

"God made man only a little lower than the angels," in so far as He "put all things under his feet"; and man approximates indefinitely to the Divine ideal of personality in the measure that he raises himself higher and higher above nature by knowledge and self-control.

But it is first within himself that man comes in conflict with this mechanism; with uniformities of instinct and habit; with psychological and physiological laws that tend to wrest the government out of the hands of the spirit, and to destroy personality. For in virtue of his bodily organism man is a part of nature and continuous with nature,—a wheel in the universal machine. He must, then, master nature within himself, as well as outside himself—a mastery that demands difficult self-knowledge, laborious self-discipline. When we remember that virtues and vices are both classified as "habits," it is plain that a habit as such is neither good nor evil. A good habit is a psychological mechanism that frees our personality for fuller and wider action, that extends our control over nature within or outside ourselves; whereas an evil habit impedes our freedom and narrows the possibilities of life. Conditioned as we are, the same mechanism of nature or habit which can impede us and destroy our personality is also the necessary means of our spiritual development. If our struggle is against the domination of dead uniformity, law, habit, mechanism, it is only because such laws and habits, once perhaps useful, have become mischievous through changing exigencies and the demands of a fuller and higher life; because the virtues of childhood may be vices in manhood; or because these laws cross and interfere with one another, and need an adjustment of their claims. But the whole aim of our struggle is the constitution of a higher and better system of laws: not the destruction, but the reconstruction of the habit-mechanism. The very inertia and blind persistence which we have to overcome is necessary to the perpetuity and stability of the fruits of victory. That old self which has to be moulded into the new, though blind and dead, has in its day been shaped by life and intelligence, and bears their traces, as a mindless mechanism bears the traces of the mind that devised it. So, too, in the physical world the principle of death is also a condition of life. The determinism of Nature, with her system of fixed laws, of uniformities of grouping and sequence, is itself the work of Spirit,—the gathered fruit of its past victories,—and yet its blind conservatism makes it the foe of Spirit so far as it not merely retains past modifications, but in doing so resists further developments, yielding only to vigorous and reiterated onslaughts of the Will. Hence the complex character of our sentiment towards Nature as towards something at once blind and intelligent, cruel and kind, coarse and tender, forceful and feeble, sublime and despicable.

As long as life lasts there is need of this work of self-reform. Every new attainment involves higher and more complex tasks; just as every industrial invention saves labour in one way only to employ it more extensively and profitably in another. Moreover, we now understand what the old ascetics had ascertained empirically, that not to advance is to recede; that there is no standing still in the moral and spiritual life. For, like machinery, habits quickly become out of date and act as a clog on progress, unless they are continually adjusted to suit growing exigencies. When virtue gets to routine it is on the road to vice. So far as our conduct is shaped by virtue and habit, it is shaped passively; it is not active in the full spiritual sense. Yet we must deliberately commit a great deal of it to the machinery of habit or second nature, if we are to free our best energies for higher and fuller action and origination. But if we turn the means to an end, and think to rest in habituality and routine, the spirit falls asleep and ceases to be conscious and self-determining.

The ceaseless task of our inward life lies in ever moulding the natural or psychic self into an obedient instrument of the growing needs of the spirit; ever bringing " my will " into conformity with " Thy Will ": ever lessening the relative distance between one and the other under pain of seeing it spontaneously increasing; and thus to go on from strength to strength in respect of personality and self-determination.

It might at first sight seem as if this spiritual will-strength were something morally colourless, like health or wealth; something that might be used well or ill. For apparently some of the strongest characters seem to have been of the psychic type; while many who live largely on the spirit-plane are only feebly self-determining. It is this seeming fact that has led modern Goths to the worship of the strong, self-assertive type of character, of the man who curbs and mortifies his passions, who goes through fire and water, in the pursuit of his ambition, or his revenge, or his love; who sweeps down everything and every one to make a straight path to his end. Such egoistic ends are not reached without great mental and moral exertion and self-sacrifice, such as would make a Saint, Martyr, or Confessor, if expended in the service of an over-individual or spiritual interest. Yet closely examined, this strength is not true will-strength; it is the strength of passion, not of action; the strength of a rock that is hurled, not of the giant who hurls it. Admirable it may be in its own order, as are all natural forces at play however terrible, or as is all passion, so it be true passion:

> All emotion,
> Whether of gods or men; all loves and passions
> Are of two kinds; they are either informed by Wisdom,
> To reason obedient—or they are unconducted
> Flames of the burning life. The brutes of earth
> And Pan their master know these last; the first
> Are seen in me (Athene); betwixt the extremes there lie
> Innumerable alloys, and all of evil.[1]

[1] *Demeter*—Robert Bridges.

What we really admire in heroic egoism is the force of an ambition or love which so dominates and enslaves a man as to press not only his other passions, but even his reason and best spiritual energies into its service. But none the less he is a slave and not a free, self-determining agent as regards the ultimate motives of his life. He may have learnt to discipline his mind and conquer his other passions, but he has not conquered himself, his psychic, natural self. It is only the conquest of passion by passion; the domination of one form of egoistic self-will over all the rest. Freedom demands that the ultimate and dominating motive of our life should not be imposed upon us by nature, but should be self-imposed by our own spiritual choice and action; that we should hold to it by our own effort, rather than be passive in its grasp. It is by such a free effort that we hold to and appropriate the Divine Will, the universal over-individual interests of the spiritual self. And just because it is the act of our free effort, and because our grasp grows weary and trembles, true self-mastery and will-strength are far rarer and more difficult of attainment than their spurious counterfeits. As it is easier to be consistently worldly-wise than heavenly-wise, so it is easier to be thorough and strong in the psychic interest than in the spiritual interest. In the former case the working energy is given to us, nor can we resist it; in the latter we have to make it and sustain it. But if the children of light show up badly compared with the children of the world in point of thoroughness and consistency, yet such strength as they have is true strength, and their failures are due to the greater difficulty of their aim rather than to the greater slackness of their efforts. Doubtless half-and-half results, neither hot nor cold, neither very good nor very bad, are multiplied by the upward endeavour: and frank egoism and self-worship would give a higher percentage of forcible natures. But in every department progress is at the cost of great waste of material and of many failures; and the economy which grasps at immediate results of a lower kind is invariably self-defeating. What is but struggling to birth, or just new-born, is always crude, feeble, and helpless beside that which is adult or senescent; yet the former is heir of the future, while the latter will soon be of the past.

3

The endeavour to subject the psychic and natural to the spirit-life; to reproduce the Divine Will ever more fully in man here upon earth; to attain to ever higher degrees of personality, freedom, and self-determination, is the essence, rule, and justification of Christian asceticism, which, far from destroying or maiming, aims at strengthening and building up human nature into something over-human and divine. Of the wilful "destruction of the flesh" as essentially evil, of hostility to nature as such, there is no trace in Him who was the Word made flesh. For Him, the blind "will to live," the tumultuous, psychic instincts of self-preservation, self-assertion, self-expansion, the lawless forces of nature within and outside us, were as indifferent morally as the raging of the sea or the scorching of the flame. It was only from the attitude of the spirit toward them, resisting or yielding, commanding or serving, that they could borrow a moral character of good or evil. Like Himself, they were set for the rise and fall of many; for a principle of discernment and judgment; for the use or abuse; for life or death.

Yet with all this His call was to a sterner mortification and austerity than men had yet learnt—that mortification which is the essential condition of all strenuous mental and moral development; of the life of perfect reason; of the subjection of the psychic will to the spiritual and divine. It was not the mortification of the oriental ascetic, sought directly for its own sake, dictated by a disbelief in nature and in life, but such as was incidental to, and inseparable from, the quest of the highest, widest, and fullest life. "He was obedient unto death, even the death of the Cross"—obedience, conformity to the Divine Will, was the end; the Cross was but the inevitable incident: Death for Life's sake, not Death for Death's sake.

While pagan asceticism laid the chief emphasis on the external acts of abstinence or endeavour, the Christian is taught to value them chiefly as manifestations of an inward spiritual power of self-determination and mastery. It is not the act, but the power, of abstaining that matters. Actual abstinence may be a question of a particular vocation or duty, but the power of abstaining must be the aim of all. Nor is a temperate and moderate use ethically or spiritually worthful if the power of greater restraint be absent. However harmless otherwise, action which slips from the due control of our spirit becomes evil for us. And in this we touch upon that inwardness which essentially distinguishes Christian from non-Christian asceticism.

It was the failure to seize this vital and critical point that perverted the early Christian doctrine of chastity into the heresy of the Encratites. The control of the two strongest, most lawless, and socially subversive instincts of our psychic nature, *sc.* those of procreation and self-preservation, was the most evident and striking triumph of the spirit of Christ in the midst of pagan corruption. In a sense chastity is the very basis of virility and character. Here, more obviously and forcibly than in the case of any other instinctive tendency, the contrast between the psychic self-regarding aspect of the impulse and the spiritual and universal aspect is presented to us. Nowhere is it made more plain that if Nature urges us imperiously to seek ourselves, yet it is only for the sake of others; that we should regulate the impulse in accordance with her social aims; that we should correct the roughness of her expedient in the light of an intelligent appreciation of its purpose, and modify the mechanism of inborn habit into conformity with the demands of reason. And if it is sometimes objected by outsiders that chastity is not merely the basis, but the sum and substance of Catholic ethics, to the practical neglect of all else, we might reply that in this we are at least true to type, and that a like objection might have been urged against the Christians of the sub-Apostolic age. Externally, and apart from its motives, that early enthusiasm for virginity and absolute continence might easily have been, and was often, confounded with like phenomena in the religions of the East. Gnostic interpretations of Christian practice were only too frequent; and even St. Paul speaks already of fanatics "forbidding to marry and commanding to abstain from meats." But what the Christian valued in continence was the spirit which gave men power to become the sons of God; which set all things under their feet, even the winds and waves of their stormiest passions; which gifted them with a freedom and self-determination that made them more than men.

To marry or not to marry was a question of expediency; but chastity, the *power* of abstention, was obligatory on all, whether married or unmarried. In theory, the Christian Church still asserts this obligation for those thousands who without any special call to the priestly or religious state are, through circumstances of youth, poverty, deformity, sickness, disease, and the like, in a state of enforced celibacy, permanent or temporary; nor even is marriage supposed in any way to justify or allow a lesser *power* of self-control in diminishing the occasions of its exercise. Deny the universality of the obligation, and a false ethical assumption overwhelms us with insoluble social problems. Affirm and insist upon it, and we cut away the root of endless miseries and injustices that spring from the lower and laxer standard of Christian character that a mistaken indulgence has largely allowed to prevail in deference to average morality. Apart from morbid psychological conditions, inherited or induced, the *power* of abstinence is possible for all, and obligatory on all; and where it is lacking, there can be no true spiritual strength or manhood, but at most a psychic counterfeit. One lawless instinct destroys the unity of character, the perfection of freedom and self-determination. It introduces or tolerates a pseudo-personality side by side with the spirit, in the same inward kingdom, which at any moment may seize the reigns of government and bring all things to confusion.

The other great triumph of early Christianity was the martyr-spirit, the conquest of the fear of death, the perfect control of the instinct of self-preservation. A certain insensibility to pain and a reckless contempt of life—one's own or others'—is a mark of savagery and barbarism; of a defective sense of personality, its rights and values; of an enforced and complete subjection of the unit to the multitude. Plainly it is only in the measure that our personality, life, and work is valuable and duly valued that free self-sacrifice for others and for the Will of God possesses positive moral significance. Of such sacrifice Christ is the realized ideal. In a sense, none ever loved His life more, and yet none ever loved it less. Readiness to die for the Gospel was expected of all His disciples without distinction; it was not to be the special *charisma* of the comparatively few whose readiness was put to the test by martyrdom. And included in the readiness to die, as the less in the greater, was the readiness to expose oneself to the perils and occasions of death, to sacrifice health and comfort and convenience for the Gospel's sake. As in the matter of continence, so here: exultation in a new-found victory over Nature's strongest impulses often led to extravagances in the form of wanton self-destruction, demanded neither by reason nor charity and hostile to the interests of both. Later there came reaction, and an insensible process of concession to average morality. The medieval contempt of life was perhaps as much due to a recrudescence of barbarism as to the Christian spirit of fearlessness. Nowadays, when civilization has made life more sweet and death more terrible for nervous and highly developed personalities, the King of Terrors and his satellites are feared as perhaps never before. To live anyhow, at any price, by any operation or artifice, without any reference to the interest of others, and as long as possible, is widely assumed to be an unlimited right and even an unlimited duty. Fortunately the military profession is still with us to remind us of a principle which surely has wider, more general, and perhaps more rational applications; and even the deservedly obsolete practice of duelling at least taught men to make light of death in comparison with the moral evil of dishonour. Not only in the defence of one's country or of one's personal honour, but in a multitude of fairly ordinary contingencies, the preservation of our own life may not be that supreme and absolute end that we think it, and there may be something quite analogous to incontinence in the unrestrained eagerness with which we cling to it; an eagerness which belongs to the psychic rather than to the spiritual man.

4

Nothing is more possible, probable, or common than to find the direct pursuit of self-denial as an end in itself co-existing with a total neglect of the daily and multitudinous self-denials incident to the perfect discharge of our duty. There is no asceticism so severe, so exigent, so humble and humbling as that involved in perfect fidelity to reasonableness. As in the government of others, so in that of ourselves, arbitrariness is always uneducative and demoralizing. " Because I choose" is never a reason ; or it is one which justly brings a government into discredit and eventually leads to its overthrow. We must not give senseless orders to ourselves any more than to others. Our will is not a plaything, and if we use it as such we destroy it. Mortifications that are mere will-feats, and are not directed in some way to the service of reason, only feed vanity at the expense of character. Of such asceticism Christ knows nothing. Yet the call to follow Him is incidentally and inevitably a call to take up the Cross, to deny oneself daily and hourly ; to labour in the sweat of one's brow ; to wrestle with the tough resistance of nature and habit ; to discipline one's mind and imagination, one's senses, feelings, passions, affections ; to withstand the forces that split up and disintegrate one's personality ; to organize and unify the lawless multitude of our thoughts, aims, and tendencies ; to bring all under the absolute control of the Divine Will.

This is a task not for the weak, but for the strong ;

for those who "go on from strength to strength"; who do violence to themselves and so take the Kingdom of Heaven by storm; not for reeds shaken by the wind, nor for those who are clothed in soft raiment and live in the palaces of kings. If the Crucifix breathes tranquillity in the midst of pain, it is the tranquillity of a hard-won conquest, the fruit of Gethsemane's agony and sweat of blood. Nor without innumerable agonies of prayer and repugnance can the psychic and natural self be subjected to the spiritual or the Christian type of manhood—free, strong, self-determining—be realized, sustained, and furthered; or God's Will be done in earth, as it is in heaven. "The spirit, indeed, is willing, but the flesh is weak": to change this weakness into strength is the work of the spirit which appropriates and identifies itself with the Divine Will.

5

Heaven is the abode of eternal peace and rest; the assembly of spirits in whom the Divine Will is finally triumphant. But it is the rest of action, not of inertia or slumber. In our present militant condition, labour is so invariably painful that we can hardly dissociate the two ideas. Yet closer reflection shows us that vacancy and under-exertion are as painful as the overtaxing of our energies, and that our fullest joy, our truest rest, is in the adequate exercise of our best faculties. But such exercise, whether of the mind or the will or the body, necessarily implies an obstacle to be encountered and overcome. The sense of insecurity, the uncertainty of immediate victory, are not altogether limitations of our flesh. In due measure they are a stimulus, a condiment; yet the possibility of ultimate defeat and failure is inconsistent with perfect peace and serenity. Till that possibility is eliminated God's Will cannot be done on earth as it is in heaven— namely, in imperturbable peace and security. Yet even on earth we may approximate to this heaven: and thus the growth of spiritual strength is marked by increasing serenity and restfulness. There is an ease that comes of habit, and there is an ease that comes of spiritual strength. The former is useful as freeing the spirit for higher tasks, but is hurtful if turned to an occasion of idleness. It is merely a self-induced perfection of the psychological mechanism fashioned by the spirit for its own service. It puts a better instrument into the workman's hands and makes his work easier, yet it does not increase his skill or industry, but only calls him to greater and higher exertion. Far other is the ease that without lessening the bitterness of the chalice, or the weakness of the flesh, increases the willingness of the spirit. Grace is essentially a spiritual help. It does not weaken or pauperize us by numbing our pain or lightening our burdens, but enables us to endure and to labour by clearing our vision and kindling our love. At every onward stage the spirit is more conscious of its nearness and dearness to God; more sensible of its communion with the Divine Life; more sure that it is in the grasp of a hand that will not let go. And with this consciousness its hope and confidence and courage approximate to that eternal rest and security which constitute heaven. The Will that moves all is in itself unmoved in the infinite intensity of its action ; and the wills that are merged in it share its rest.

"Then wilt Thou rest in our rest, even as now Thou dost labour in our labour: and, thus, as Thy working is done through us, so will Thy resting be done through us."[1]

VII

THE FOURTH PETITION

Panem nostrum quotidianum da nobis hodie.—Give us this day our daily bread

I

"Labour not," says our Lord, "for the meat that perisheth, but for the meat that endureth unto everlasting life." What this imperishable meat is He tells us elsewhere: "I have a meat ye know not of. My meat is to do the will of Him that sent Me"; and for this meat He has taught us to pray: "Thy Will be done on earth, as it is in heaven."

The spirit has its hunger. "Blessed are they that hunger after righteousness." That it can desire, as its own good and satisfaction, the Kingdom of God and the Will of God, shows us that it identifies itself with God, and has nothing individual or selfish in its nature, but rises above the psychic plane and loses itself in God ; that it is by destiny an organ in which the Divine Will and Life expresses itself; in which God wills, and loves, and acts. Only because it

[1] "Aug. Conf." XIII. 37.

freely identifies itself with God, and dies into God, can it possibly regard the universal over-individual interests of truth and justice as its own interests, since the nature of the object desired explains the nature of the subject who desires it. Only because it can, at moments, take the absolute standpoint and see with God's eyes can it also become conscious of the relativity and falseness of the psychic, the autocentric, standpoint. If the contemplation of stellar spaces dwarf us in our self-esteem, the fact that we can be so dwarfed means that we stand outside, or are greater than, the terms compared—the psychic self and the material universe.

God's Will, God's Kingdom, is the bread of man's eternal life—the life in which he identifies himself with the Eternal. Not merely does it satisfy his spiritual hunger, but it builds up his spiritual substance. Unlike the bread of the body, which is changed into man's nature, this heavenly bread changes man into its own nature. In the measure that he appropriates the Divine Life and Will, he puts on divinity. He feeds on a higher nature than his own, not on a lower. Assimilation requires here that he, and not his nutriment, should be transformed. It is a life ready made, like that of the civilization into which we are born. To appropriate it we must not narrow or lower it to the compass of our faculties, but widen and raise our faculties to take it in as it is. Our civilization may be improved, and, after we have compassed it, we may criticize and amend it; but we cannot improve on the Divine Life,—we have only to receive it.

The first and principal part of the Lord's Prayer is preoccupied with the Bread of the Spirit, the meat that endureth ; the second and dependent part with the meat that perisheth, the bread of the body. The first, with spiritual interests ; the second, with psychic or natural interests in relation to these : " Seek ye first the Kingdom of God and His righteousness, and all these things shall be added unto you."

Bread stands in this petition for the satisfaction of all the needs of our natural life,—for food and raiment and housing, and all those things " which the Gentiles seek," and seek wrongly only so far as they seek them out of due order and measure, and without respect to the one thing absolutely needful. And the selfish greed of this bread is the root and occasion of all those sins and trespasses for which we ask forgiveness, and which we have to forgive in others ; and of the temptation to sin from which we desire to be guarded ; and of the vices and evils from which we pray to be delivered.

2

The house of man's heart is never vacant. Either good or evil spirits must make their abode there. Drive out one devil, and another will forthwith enter, unless the Spirit of God have taken possession already. Merely negative reformation is futile ; unless evil be driven out by the intrusion of good, and error by the intrusion of truth, they will return in some other form, and the last state may be worse than the first.

It was not in void space that Christ came to

establish the Kingdom of God, but in an occupied territory where Satan had established his usurped throne. He had "to destroy the works of the devil" in order "to make us sons of God." Yet He did not first destroy and then build up, but destroyed by building up. By forcing Himself in, He forced Satan out.

In the Gospel the Kingdom of God and the Kingdom of Satan are correlative ideas which explain one another. The first part of the Lord's Prayer is occupied with the Kingdom of God; the second with the Kingdom of Satan, with the world, the flesh, and the devil, with concupiscence and sin and temptation. When the Tempter drew nigh to Our Lord in the desert, the first snare that he spread was the commonest, the most widely destructive. "If Thou be the Son of God, command these stones to become bread." It was an appeal to those elementary and imperative needs of the psychic man whose inordinate quest is the most abundant source of human sin and suffering. "Not by bread alone," says Christ, "shall man live, but by every word that proceedeth out of the mouth of God"; not by the meat which perisheth, but by the meat which endureth.

The psychic appetites and desires are as real and positive as the hunger and thirst after righteousness. They are forces which should be curbed and brought under the service of the spirit, and as such they are constitutive of the Kingdom of God—of the reign of order. But left to themselves they act blindly, and make for chaos and confusion, and as such they are constitutive of the Kingdom of Satan—of the reign of disorder. We must not think of evil, or the principles of evil, as merely negative; or of the Kingdom of Satan as an unoccupied waste, or as the merely embryonic unfinished stage of "good in the making." We should view it as the moral chaos produced by uncurbed egotism; by the unbridled freedom of instincts made for service and not for freedom; by the innate propensity of each psychic unit to make itself central and supreme, and to subject every other unit to its own separate and exclusive interests; by the intrusion of the natural law of competition into the spiritual domain. If the result to some extent is merely destructive of order, subversive of the Kingdom of God, yet the destroying forces are as positive as the powers of good. Nor can we altogether say that the reign of evil is lawless. "If Satan be divided against Satan, how can his kingdom stand?" There is system and stability in the world of selfishness. As we have said already, the psychic life produces a civilization of its own, and the psychic man, dominated by some enslaving ambition or desire, can reach a degree of seeming personality and self-command which the spiritual man often misses. It is not merely blind passions and instincts that war against divine order, but reason and the laws of nature are pressed into their service and organize their forces for the battle. Were it otherwise, they would be at once what they must be eventually, "chaff before the wind"; whereas now the conflict is between kingdom and kingdom, order and order—between the real and the apparent, the true and the false.

Man must have bread: in a sense, it is his first need—first in order of time, and counting from below. He is earthly and psychic before he becomes heavenly and spiritual. *Non mortui laudabunt Te,* "The dead cannot praise Thee"; we must live in the body if we are to live to God. Hence the external Kingdom of Heaven on earth postulates rational conditions of bodily subsistence for all. Where these are lacking, or where they superabound, man is tempted to live for bread alone. Destitution and superfluity alike, though in contrary ways, are disorders of the Kingdom of Satan.

The Kingdom of Satan, like that of God, has its inward and its outward aspect. Primarily it means the reign of selfishness in the hearts of mankind at large. Secondarily it means all those conditions of human society which both foster and result from this inward evil.

In the Gospel we find the ills of soul and body indifferently ascribed to Satan. Sickness is assumed to be the fruit of sin; the only problem being: Who has sinned: this man or his parents? Our Lord is the Physician of soul and body indiscriminately; that is, of the whole man; of all sickness, moral or physical. To cure the paralytic of his infirmity and to forgive his sins are equally "to destroy the works of the devil." It is Satan who has bound that daughter of Abraham for eighteen years in her infirmity.

We may explain details differently in these days, but the main fact of the causal relation between the inward life and the outward conditions of mankind in general is uncontestable. These latter may proceed from sin and make for sin; or they may proceed from righteousness and make for righteousness; they may constitute a visible Kingdom of Satan or a visible Kingdom of God.

It is to the disorder of man's fundamental and necessary instinct of self-nourishment, self-care, self-protection, that the origin of all sin and of the Kingdom of Satan is traced in the teaching of the Sacred Scriptures—to the temptation to live by bread alone and not by every word that proceedeth from the mouth of God; to an abandonment of the spiritual plane, with its selfless universal interests, and a descent to the psychic plane, with its selfish interests.

3

Those fishermen who listened to our Lord, the first to whom He taught this prayer, were poor men, and therefore more exposed to the spiritual dangers of destitution and insufficiency than to those of superfluity. Their temptations were not those of the rich men of the parables, whom ease and indulgences had blinded to the life-problems raised by the experience of suffering and sorrow. As destructive of such indolent contentment and optimism, poverty or even destitution is a grace: Blessed are ye poor. Luxurious conditions have never originated any high degree of civilization and have invariably destroyed what has been built up by the pressure of need and stress. And this is true of religion—the highest factor of civilization. It is a shallow scoff that speaks of calamity sending man howling to his gods. Undoubtedly it is the stress of man's spiritual and moral needs, his painful limitations and necessities, his radical and incurable discontent with all that a godless world offers, or could be conceived to offer, that forces him to believe in a bigger world in which the puzzles of our fragmentary experience find their solution. Woe, therefore, to the rich who slumber comfortably through life without a jolt or jar to wake them from dreams to realities; and blessed are the poor, whom suffering presses with questions that faith alone can answer.

Still there is a degree of poverty which absorbs all the leisure and best energies of life in the struggle for bare subsistence, which tends to harden and sterilize the spirit, and which creates habits of greed and grasping that often persist after the pressure is removed and tie the soul down to the service of Mammon. Against such a snare we are taught to pray, "Give us this day our daily bread"—a prayer which at once recognizes our lawful bodily desires and the limits within which they should be contained.

"Your Heavenly Father knoweth that you have need of these things." Neither does He need to be informed of our wants, or to be persuaded to satisfy them. What He requires of us is an acknowledgment of dependence; a sense of confidence in, and resignation to, the rulings of His providence; a conforming of our wills to His, not a wresting of His will to ours.

We are told that He who clothes the lilies will surely clothe us; that He who feeds the sparrows will surely feed us. But to find in these words an encouragement to idleness and improvidence is unpardonable. When we pray, "Thy Kingdom come," we pray for grace to desire and work for its coming; when we pray, "Give us this day our daily bread," we pray that we may be able to procure it by our own endeavour. The sparrows are not fed miraculously, but work hard for their food; and in the frost and snow they perish in their thousands. Yet it is God, working in the laws of nature, who feeds them; and when, in obedience to those same laws, they fall to earth and perish, it is not without their Heavenly Father's will. The fishermen of Galilee well knew that they had to spread their nets and toil all night if they were to take the bounty that God might or might not send them. The field-labourers knew that they must plough, sow, and reap, though it was for God to give the increase. Both knew that their daily bread depended on their own labour as well as on God's gifts; that it was idle to pray except with the intention of working. Prayer looks to those conditions of success without which all our labour and foresight would be vain; which depend on what, in relation to our ignorance and helplessness, we call luck or chance, and what, in relation to our faith, we call providence—on rain and sunshine, storm and calm. To pray is to utter our firm faith that the whole mechanism of nature is in God's hands; that its laws and necessities are subservient to His will; that seeming evil, no less than seeming good, is co-operant to wise and loving ends. It is to resign ourselves, after we have done our part, to whatever the wheel of fortune brings round to our lot—not with the stolidity of the fatalist, but with the obedience of a child, perplexed by the rulings of a fatherly wisdom which is beyond its powers of comprehension and criticism. In spite of the implied dualism which represents God as being, manwise, in conflict with nature and unable to secure His ends except through ceaseless interventions with an order He finds established, there is deeper truth in the naïve faith that prays for such miracles than in the dumb, sullen resignation of oneself to the senseless control of an ultimate and all-pervading mechanism. For it is to believe that God is stronger than nature; that He is transcendent as well as immanent; that nature is a first habit, even as habit is a second nature, and that therefore, like habit, nature is created and moulded by intelligence and will. But to believe that this mechanism itself is the chosen instrument through which the Divine Love and Freedom shape our ends, to believe that Law and Liberty are reconcilable—is a yet deeper faith which absorbs the truth and rejects the error of these imperfect views of providence. This higher faith will not dare to dictate or urge, or to judge what is expedient or otherwise, but commends itself blindly into God's hands, praying only, "Not my will, but Thine be done." As it will not repine if its desires be thwarted, so neither will it be elated when they are gratified; for this too would be to claim to know what we can never know, namely, which of the two is ultimately the better for us—

affliction or prosperity. To see God's finger only in wonderful coincidences and answers to prayer implies an unconscious denial of intervention where we do not see it. "If we have received good things as from God's hands, shall we not also receive evil?" The truest faith *knows* His finger is in everything, but *sees* it in nothing: "Because thou hast seen, thou hast believed. Blessed are they that have not seen, and yet have believed."

Plainly, what Christ forbids is not a rational and moderated care for the indispensable conditions of life, but such a solicitude or absorption as forgets the end in the means, and thrusts the Kingdom of God into the second place. It is not so much what "the Gentiles seek" that is reprehended, as the manner in which they seek it.

We need not stay to dispute the exact meaning of "epiousios" (daily). The rendering "supersubstantial" is so utterly improbable on philological grounds, and so subversive of the sequence and connexion that gives the prayer its unity, that we may pass it by. The other renderings agree in their ultimate sense; that is, they preclude vain anxiety about future contingencies which lie beyond all possible human knowledge and control; and they enjoin that necessary trust in providence which in no right sense can be stigmatized as improvidence. The morrow for which we are to take no thought is not regulated by the sun, but lies beyond that night of ignorance which inevitably bounds our foresight. It is the hidden and uncontrollable future. But there is also enjoined upon us a sort of unworldliness much more akin to improvidence. Our Lord was immediately addressing those whom He was sending forth, as sheep into the midst of wolves, to preach the Gospel of the coming Kingdom; who would therefore be constantly confronted with alternatives between principle and expediency, between truth and the cost of truth, right and the cost of right. Here are the moments, not rare in any life, when one must blind oneself to consequences and plunge; when to hesitate or look back is to prove oneself unfit for the Kingdom of God. *Fiat justitia, ruat cælum.* This so-called "improvidence" distinguishes the spiritual from the psychic or natural man, and constitutes that folly of the Cross which is wisdom with God.

Yet even short of this, Christian wisdom forbids an infinite carefulness that would in every case strain foresight to its utmost limits without respect to the varying importance of the matters in question; that would sickly o'er the native hue of resolution with the pale cast of thought, and waste golden opportunity through lack of firmness and promptitude. This is less often an error of the worldly-wise than of the scrupulous and conscientious. And therefore we need to be reminded that though we ourselves are responsible, God is also responsible; that risk is inseparable from choice and action; that it is safer to lose five talents through boldness than to save one by timidity.

Finally, belief in the almost immediate end of the world justified the early Christians in an indifference to many temporal concerns that would otherwise have been an inexcusable improvidence. Who would trouble about his clothing, housing, and sustenance in future years were he doomed to die in a month or two? If at all times a deeper sense of life's brevity and littleness makes the true Christian more calm under temporal losses and afflictions, and mitigates that intensity of competition for subsistence and enjoyment which comes of a narrow and exaggerated estimate of the prizes, this surely is not improvidence, but a wiser and wider foresight that rates more justly the relation of the means to the end. To care too little is bad; but to care too much is far worse. From this over-care faith delivers us, in that it tells us that for each, if not for all, not only death but judgment is near—even at the very gates. It presses us with the same spiritual truth which for the early Christians was embodied in the belief that the world itself was in its agony.

4

Our Heavenly Father knows that we have need of these temporal things and that our neighbour has need of them—need of everything that ministers to the elevation of man to ever higher spiritual planes; need of all that is meant by a rational civilization, by the external Kingdom of Heaven upon earth. And with the right and duty of praying for these ends comes the right and duty of working for them. It is to our Father in heaven that we pray for the bread of the body no less than for the bread of the soul; for He is Father of body and soul alike, of earth and Heaven; nor are these interests separable or separated but by sin. Heaven is in earth, and earth is in heaven; if the eternal transcends it also permeates the temporal.

And as we pray to "our" Father, so we pray for "our" bread in no exclusive sense; in no egotistic, self-seeking spirit which uses prayer but as another weapon in the lupine struggle for subsistence. It is a corporate prayer for a corporate need; we are looking each of us rather to the common good than to our own. We are thinking of the wants of others around us; of the outward Kingdom of God upon earth.

What is expressed in the following petition is surely implied in this. For He who has said, "Forgive, and you shall be forgiven," has also said, "Give, and it shall be given to you." He has taught us to see our Father made visible in our brother, and thrown upon our mercy and compassion. As it is vain to approach His altar with gifts unless we be first reconciled to our brother, so, too, if our brother be starving, no "Corban" casuistry will buy us off this more pressing and imperative form of sacrifice. If need be, let His servants be fed with the showbread from the sacred table itself. Will He delight in vessels of gold when the living vessels of His service are perishing and neglected? But again, it is presumption and superstition to pray for the general needs of our brethren if we are not minded to work for them, and to devote ourselves, heart and soul, according to our ability, to what are called "social problems." Those of our day were not dreamt of, could not have been formulated or understood, in

Judæa two thousand years ago. To look for their key in the Gospels is folly and fanaticism. But the great end and the great motive of all social endeavour are essential determinants of the spirit of Christ. More than this, the Gospel of Poverty, sanely interpreted, strikes at the most abiding and universal sources of social misery, and shakes the strongest supports of Satan's throne. The greed of superfluity in the few is largely answerable for the destitution of the many. There is a rational use of wealth and an irrational waste of wealth. The latter, not the former, is the sin of the rich, and the cause of the impoverishment of the community as a whole. Society is not poorer but richer, when a man spends his needless wealth on jewellery or curiosities; but if he flings it in the sea, or hoards it in the earth, or uses his library for fuel, or employs labour fruitlessly, he is eventually taking bread out of the mouths of the poor and furthering destitution.

The Gospel teaches a doctrine of frugality when it bids us seek one thing alone, without restraint or measure, and all else with a certain severity of moderation, in reference and subordination to that; when it bids us regulate our ends hierarchically, seeking the lower in sufficiency for the higher and no more. It introduces an æsthetic principle into life that condemns the vulgarity of every sort of profusion or waste, and secures a sort of Greek elegance of just proportion.

Certain advocates of "the simple life" would claim Gospel authority for a vandalism that levels all social inequalities of wealth and possession and robs life of that unity in variety which is of its essence. The simplicity of uniformity and monotony is the cheapest, but it is not the best. That best is attained when the sovereign end of life controls the infinite variety of means; when each member of the social organism perfects itself for its own place and function solely in the interests of the whole; in a word, when the psychic man is subject to the spiritual.

VIII

THE FIFTH PETITION

Dimitte nobis debita nostra, sicut et nos dimittimus debitoribus nostris.—Forgive us our trespasses, as we forgive them that trespass against us.

I

We may leave the whole problem of freedom and of the possibility and permission of sin aside, and accept the fact that in the world, as at present constituted, sin abounds and superabounds; that man's need of forgiveness is as universal as his need of food and clothing. The root of all sin is the lusting of the flesh against the spirit; of the psychic against the spiritual self. It lies in the blind lawlessness of those self-assertive instincts which, kept in due subjection, are the indispensable instruments of spiritual development and self-manifestation. Yet it is the spirit that sins, and not the flesh. The spirit not only may, but must identify itself with the interest of its servant—of the individual organism which it controls. The actor who puts himself in another's place becomes that other for the time being, and dies to his normal self. So, too, the spirit has continually to assume the interests of the body, to clothe itself with material individuality, to become a psychic self for the time being. Only by rapid alternations between the spiritual rôle and the psychic can it adjust the naturally conflicting interests of both sides. In each rôle it experiences a different set, or order, of pains and pleasures, revulsions and attractions. Hence, a certain division of personality is normal and necessary; we will and we do not will; we hope and we fear one and the same end or object; and if never in precisely the same psychological instant, yet a flutter of alternations gives an illusion of simultaneity. The spirit sins when it abandons itself to the psychic rôle, to the neglect of the spiritual; when it suffers itself to be swayed passively where it should actively command; when it yields itself to the blind laws of individual self-assertion and self-supremacy. Sin is the schism of the spirit from the harmony of wills in communion with the Divine Will—its apostasy from the spiritual to the psychic order, from the Kingdom of God to the Kingdom of Satan, from charity to egoism. The consequent sense of guilt is a sense of antagonism to the ultimately irresistible forces of goodness and truth; a sense of identification with a doomed cause; of loss of that personality which is measured by power over nature and appropriation of the divine life and strength. The spirit fallen from grace or charity withers and rots as a branch torn from the Tree of Life.

2

The union of wills through love is a mutual relation. An unreturned love on either side is not enough. If the outstretched hand is not grasped there is no bond between soul and soul. It needs a free act on the part both of the offender and of the offended to bridge over the breach; on the part of the former, repentance; on the part of the latter, forgiveness. Forgiveness, however, is a duty in the same sense in which love—the first and great commandment — is a duty: and therefore the offender has a right to our forgiveness as he has to our love. To refuse forgiveness is an offence against the offender and against God; one that shuts us out from the Communion of Saints till we ourselves repent and learn to win mercy by mercy.

Sin is the violation, forgiveness the restoration, of that will-union with God and His saints in which the spirit-life consists,—of that union which is symbolized and cemented by those sacramental acts in which we receive and are received by the mystical Christ; in which we profess to be, and are acknowledged as, sons of God, members of a divine organism.

This union is the Kingdom of God, the sovereign end of the Divine Will in all its outward workings: "He that cometh unto Me I will in no wise cast out." God could not refuse forgiveness to the penitent without a violation of His essential goodness. "As I live, I desire not the death of a sinner, but rather that he be converted and live."

But this conversion or penitence means a return

of the old love, a recovery of the abandoned spiritual plane, a condemnation of the selfishly psychic standpoint. Such spiritual repentance implies an already accomplished restoration to spiritual life and Divine Sonship, so that the grace of repentance and the grace of forgiveness are but two aspects of one thing. The purely contrite soul, whose contrition is selfless and disinterested, is already forgiven. It has no need to pray for forgiveness. To pray for forgiveness, therefore, is to pray for the grace of contrition, for power to repent and love.

The spirit-life, as has been said, is not evolved out of ourselves, as a tree from the seed, but is offered to us for our appropriation. It does not lie within ourselves to love or to repent, as though we had only ourselves to thank. If, while breath remains, God's hand is always stretched out to the fallen, it is not the less an act of love and grace on His part. Uniformity is not necessity. We could not pray for forgiveness had He not already begun the work of repentance in our hearts; and here the parable of divine forgiveness breaks down hopelessly, for the sinner cannot so much as wish to return home "unless the Father draw him."

Still, forgiven though we be, we can pray for forgiveness, not only in view of ever possible future offences, but with respect to those already pardoned. For as spiritual life and love admit of endless increase, so also do the repentance and forgiveness which they carry along with them. "Wash me more and more from my wickedness," says the Psalmist, recognizing that divine purity is no mere negation, like that of the body; that the soul may be whiter than snow, and whiter than that again, without end or limit.

Moreover, the prayer to our common Father is not personal or particular in any exclusive sense, but universal and in the name of all. It was the prayer of the sinless Lamb of God, who came to take away the sins of the world ; who made Himself one with His sinful brethren, and as such could say, " Forgive us our trespasses." We pray, therefore, not merely for our own repentance, but for the conversion and repentance of the world.

3

What we pray for we must work for; we pray that we may work. Our Saviour's whole Life and Passion was at once a praying and a working for the repentance of mankind ; and round that central sacrifice all our sacrifices of prayer and effort are gathered into one corporate self-oblation for the same end.

God desires that all should repent and live ; but He gives effect to this all-saving Will through the instrumentality of man, through those in whom He lives and works vicariously on earth. In these His goodness and lovableness reveal themselves and invite sinners to repentance. But in Jesus Christ these nebulous and scattered lights of revelation are gathered into a central sun: "God so loved the world, that He gave His only begotten Son, that all who believe in Him might not perish, but might have eternal life." He is uniquely and pre-eminently the Resurrection and the Life, who has power to wake the spiritually dead, already corrupted in the tomb. "He that hath seen Me hath seen the Father." In Him God shows Himself as loving sinners even to the extremity of death. In Christ crucified repentance and eternal life are proffered to us with a persuasiveness that cannot be surpassed. "Greater love hath no man than this, that a man lay down his life for his friends." Yet it is God and not man who, in Christ, lays down His life, not for His friends, but for enemies. Thus "the love of Christ constraineth us" to repentance, and thereby reconciles us with the Father and quickens us to eternal life.

And in this atoning work the members of His mystical body are called to co-operate. Not only must they pray for sinners, but by their self-sacrificing Christliness of life and character invite them to repentance and communion with God.

4

In the external and sacramental penance of the Church, Confession follows Contrition and precedes Absolution. In the spiritual and timeless world the three are coincident. Repentance is a self-accusation in the presence of the Father, who seeth in secret; it is a prayer for forgiveness which is answered before it is made. The self-accusing habit of mind is an indispensable condition of spiritual growth; it is a part of that general teachableness and receptivity without which the spirit is intractable in the hands of God. The infallible and the unteachable are doomed to stagnation and petrifaction. "If we say that we have no sin, we deceive ourselves, and the truth is not in us." As necessarily as prayer tends to embody itself in utterance, and requires utterance for its due development, so necessarily does contrition require confession and the deeds of penance—not merely such deeds as are due already by a thousand titles, but deeds done more abundantly, humbly, and diligently to redeem the time that is lost by past sin and negligence. The spirit-life for us sinners is essentially, a penitential life—and it is such for us collectively, and in view of our corporate transgressions, no less than individually. The building up of the spirit is no work of wasteless progress, no triumphant march of reason, but a work of laborious fluctuation, of continual repair, of going back upon past faults and breaches; a picking up of missed stitches, an endeavour to turn losses into gains, and to weave our very sins into a garment of glory.

It is only with such penitential purposes in our minds and for the furtherance of the same that we have a right to pray, "Forgive us our trespasses."

5

Between man and man, on the psychic or natural plane, there are relations of offence and forgiveness of a wholly different kind to those which obtain in the spiritual order. The self-interests of the self-seeking sometimes clash and sometimes coincide. The pride or avarice or passion of another offends me because it interferes with my own; the world is too small for us; there is not enough bread to go round. The dislike or hostility roused by such offence is a psychic instinct, rebellious against reason and spirit. The forgiveness accorded to such offence may be merely of the same quality, namely, psychic, self-regarding, an effect of passion rather than of action. "If ye love them that love you, what reward have you? Do not the publicans do the same? And if you salute your brethren only, what do ye more than others? Do not even the Gentiles the same?" The union effected by such friendship and forgiveness is a union in psychic, not in spiritual interests; in ends common to a few, not in those that are universal and supreme over all.

To refuse forgiveness to the duly repentant offender is to look on his offence, not in its deepest aspect as a violation of objective justice and of that Divine Will which is the supreme interest of the spirit-life, but in its aspect of opposition to our separate psychic interests. It is, therefore, to prefer the gratification of our natural self-defensive instincts to the demand of charity; it is to cut ourselves off from spiritual communion with one whose repentance has reunited him to the communion of the just with God, and therefore to excommunicate not him, but ourselves.

On the other hand, the very act of forgiveness, being an act of disinterested goodness, a denial of the psychic self for God's sake, raises us above the natural level to that of Divine Sonship, and thereby washes away our own sins.

Hence Christian forgiveness has nothing to do with the almost animal squabblings and makings-up of the unethical life. It is an exercise of heroic magnanimity; an act of the more-than-man, of the few, not of the many; a hard conquest of the psychic by the spiritual self. It is therefore by no arbitrary *fiat* of God's Will, but by the very necessities of the spiritual nature, that we cannot be forgiven unless we forgive; that we cannot forgive and not be forgiven; that when we pray to be forgiven we are praying for grace and strength to forgive.

6

Obviously the same law must govern our attitude towards the impenitent offender whose impenitence excommunicates him from the communion of the spiritually living. The last condition of forgiveness is wanting in such case on the part of the offender; but the hand of the offended must be stretched out in invitation and readiness, even as God's hand is ever stretched out to us all. The psychic instinct of vindictiveness, the egotist sense of private wrong, must be kept down and subordinated to the disinterested judgment of the spirit. If we condemn or resist or punish, it must be as though the injury affected another in no way allied with our self-interest. Our anger must be in the cause of God and justice, not in the cause of self. This surely is no child's task, no work of passive benevolence and amiability, but the deed of one who knows that the Kingdom of Heaven suffers violence and that only the violent take it by storm. Christian meekness has nothing to do with weakness. If weakness restrains the many from vengeance, strength restrains the few—those for whom it would be far easier to yield themselves passively to the tide of passion.

But besides active and wilful offence, which is comparatively rare, there is a vast deal of unconscious offensiveness on the part of our neighbour to which the spirit of forgiveness must be extended, if the like offensiveness in ourselves is to be pardoned by Him whom we pray to forgive not only our sins, but our negligences and ignorances. Nowhere is the paltriness, narrowness, and intolerance of the psychic self more difficult to control than in this matter. He indeed would be more than man and little lower than the angels who here had himself perfectly in hand; who could forgive those offensive uncongenialities of mind and manner and character and appearance which wound his self-love in a thousand ways, and which by their multiplicity are more effectual in causing division than the occasional sword-thrusts of deliberate injury.

Yet here too it is necessary by a strong effort of the spirit to rise above the psychic and individualist standpoint and to view the matter with disinterested other-regarding eyes; to judge as we would fain be judged—not flatteringly, but truthfully, and therefore mercifully—or as we should judge were we not ourselves smarting under personal irritation. Such mercy has nothing to do with the cheap optimism of an uncritical eye, a blunted moral sense, or a thick skin. 'Tis mightiest in the mightiest; it is an attribute of God Himself, an active strength, not a yielding weakness or complaisance.

Thus, not only forgiveness in the strict sense of the word, but in that wider sense which relates to the unrepentant or to the involuntary offender, is both a necessary condition and an infallible cause of that forgiveness which we need for our own offences against God; and this, because it is an act by which we are raised from the psychic to the spiritual plane and made sons of God; an act which God Himself works in us, who loves, serves, helps, and pardons man, in man, through man.

7

Plainly the heroism of the act of forgiveness is measured by the victory over feeling and instinct. But it also involves a discontent with the very rebellion of sense which demands such heroism, and a steady determination to bring habits, instincts, and feelings into accord with the spirit so as to free its energies for yet fuller and higher exercise. Condemned and disregarded, the feeling of aversion or hostility is inculpable; but forgiveness is most perfect when it is of the whole man; when self-induced habits have disciplined the psychic self to prompt and ready obedience; have sweetened the temper by an infusion of reasonableness, and schooled the easily troubled passions to an abiding serenity.

Such self-mastery is always relative and susceptible of indefinite increase, but it may frequently suffice against all ordinary occasions of perturbation. The psychic, no less than spiritual meekness and serenity of a Christ, proof against the fiercest onslaughts of injustice and the deepest insight into human limitations, demands no measured portion of the spirit, but that plenitude of divine goodness and strength before which the angriest winds and waves sink promptly to rest.

8

This takes us to the question of the difference and the relation between the spiritual and the natural love of our neighbour. It might seem that this complete victory over the psychic impulses of attraction or aversion towards others reduced Christian charity to a bloodless, calculated act of the rational will, in which the heart with its affections and feelings went for nothing. This plainly would be a dividing of the spirit and a dividing of Christ such as we have been repudiating all along. We have conceded to " Sentimentality " that the first impression made by the Gospel Christ is that of a tenderness of affection and compassion as far removed as possible from the cold charity of Stoical justice. What we deny is, the confusion of love with emotionalism; of feeling regulated and controlled by the spirit in its own service, with feeling blindly and passively obeyed.

Unregulated feeling and affection, like any psychic impulse, resembles an uncultivated vine that sprawls out in every direction, and grows poorer and weaker season by season. Pruned and restrained, its strength and fruitfulness would have been steadily augmented. The indulgent softness of indiscriminate charity of every sort, which follows the first impulse of pity, never looking to wider and more distant consequences; which dares not, when necessary, use the knife or the lash; which shrinks from the pain of inflicting pain, or of denying pleasure—is merely psychic selfishness in one of its pleasanter manifestations, a sympathy that has little to do with real costing kindness.

The spirit of Christ grapples with this lawless rabble of psychic impulses; subjects them to severe discipline, and yokes them into its chariot. It is not driven by them, but drives them. Yet it needs their service, and is helpless without them. They may writhe and smart under its lash, but they are all the better and stronger for being kept well in hand, and guided to those higher and more wide-reaching ends of love which else they had defeated.

Our duties towards others are not merely duties of action, but duties of feeling—we must not merely act, but also feel, love and forgiveness as far as feeling is in our control; and we are bound to strive continually to bring it more fully under our control, and to conform the psychic to the spiritual will. For feeling can be and is slowly educated by indulgence or by denial, and by the habitual control of the imagination. Brooding can develop a spark of dislike into a conflagration of hatred; and feelings frequently uttered in word or action strike a deeper root in the soul.

The truth that God identifies Himself with our neighbour is one of the keynotes of the Gospel: "Give, and it shall be given to you; forgive, and you shall be forgiven." Yet it is not merely because, in them, we have given to Him, and have forgiven Him, that He gives to us and forgives us; not merely as a *quid pro quo*, or as a debt or gratitude or justice, such as may be due from one individual to another whose interests can clash or coincide. It is because that in such giving and forgiving as Christ demands of us we rise above the selfish standpoint and take our place on the spiritual plane among the children of our Father in heaven, who makes His sun to shine on the evil and the good and sends His rain on the just and the unjust.

IX

THE SIXTH PETITION

Ne nos inducas in tentationem.—Lead us not into temptation

I

This petition and the following are related very much as the third and fourth. As "Thy Kingdom come" is explained by "Thy Will be done on earth," so is "Lead us not into temptation" by the plainly dependent "But deliver us from evil." Hence St. Luke omits the seventh as he does the fourth, and presumably for the same reason—that it adds nothing to the substance of the prayer.

The preceding petition for forgiveness implies a sincere detestation of sin; and this again a sincere desire, purpose, and endeavour to minimize the occasions and causes of sin. Temptations are of two kinds—those that are, morally speaking, beyond our strength, and those that are within our strength. Of the latter it is said, "Blessed is the man that endureth temptation" (James I. 12); "Count it all joy when ye fall into temptation" (*ibid*. 2); "I pray not that Thou shouldest take them out of the world" (John XVII.). Of the former: "But I pray . . that Thou shouldest keep them from evil" (John XVII.); "God will not suffer you to be tempted above what you are able" (1 Cor. X. 12); "Watch and pray, that you enter not into temptation: for the spirit is willing, but the flesh is weak" (Matt. XXVI. 41); "Lead us not into temptation, but deliver us from evil."

To strengthen the weakness of the flesh (i.e. of our psychic nature) by subjecting it to the spirit is the ever-receding goal of our moral and religious progress, which is therefore a progress in freedom and self-mastery. The limits of strength and freedom differ for man and man; and for different seasons and states of the same man. Freedom is conditioned by the clearness of our general moral judgment and insight, and by that of our judgment as to the morality of the particular act in question; by the degree of acquired or natural control over our reason, our imagination, our habits, feelings, and affections; by our immunity from distraction or surprise or sudden passion. We must know what we are doing, and why we are doing it, and that we are in no way forced to do it. The measure of our normal and habitual freedom is determined by our own moral industry on the one side, and on the other by the resistance or pliability of the particular temperament we have to contend with. It is partly a gift, partly an acquisition. "All have not the same to conquer and mortify," says à Kempis, "and one who is diligent and zealous will often be able to make more progress, even though he have more passions to contend with, than another with a kindlier temperament who is less eager after virtue" (I. c. 25). But it may happen just as often that the more industrious reaps a poorer harvest, and must be content with the just judgment of the Father, who seeth in secret, who values the industry more than the harvest, and with whom the first are often the last and the last first.

Again, our normal measure of freedom is liable to frequent perturbation and diminution, for which we are not responsible. Sickness, weariness, old age, depression, climatic changes, and a thousand accidents may cloud our judgment, tire our mind, disorder our nerves, throw us back for the time being to lower ethical levels long since abandoned, and so make us the easy prey of temptations against which we are normally invulnerable.

There may, therefore, be temptations that are too strong for us, whether relatively to our normal, or to our occasional, measure of freedom ; and in such cases sin is imputed to us by our conscience only so far as we needlessly incurred the temptation or culpably weakened ourselves, so as to be responsible for its improportion to our freedom. For here it is that the sin lies—not in yielding to necessity, but in inducing the necessity ; in entering into temptation above our strength. We are therefore told to watch and strive and pray that we may not be led into such temptations.

The prayer for our daily bread is not a prayer for miracles. We pray that we may work for it and earn it ; but also with an acknowledgment of our dependence on God's providence in the matter, and of our trust that whether He gives or denies, it is equally the will of a loving Father whose wisdom must in many ways be inscrutable to His children. So too we pray that we may strive to avoid insuperable temptations, but with an acknowledgment that our vigilance is vain if God's providence do not favour us; and with a trust that should He, as He often does, allow such evil to come upon us without our fault, He will hold us blameless and turn it all to our good. *Sortes meae in manu tua sunt*—"My lots are in Thy hand"; no movement of the world's seemingly ruthless mechanism escapes the Will of Him whose Spirit fashioned it for its own ends. "If we have received good things at His hand, shall we not also receive evil?" Clearly, then, the striving against insuperable temptations demands an outward and an inward vigilance. It demands first that we walk circumspectly, not as fools, but as wise; as pioneers in a forest where danger may lurk around, above, or under foot; that we should be sober and watchful, not reckless and foolhardy; still less, presumptuous, as those who tempt God and throw themselves headlong, relying on angelic aid promised only to those who tread cautiously should they chance to stumble. We are required to steer clear of rocks and shoals, and to this end to learn their whereabouts, profiting by our own past experiences and those of others. Still, in this there is need of that prudence which proportions the measure of vigilance to the magnitude of the danger; which checks a timidity that would paralyse our energies; which not only allows, but compels us to risk a storm rather than lie idle in port. Whatever befalls us after reasonable and proportionate care is not our own doing, but the ruling of providence, even though greater care had certainly saved us.

But it is principally by strengthening ourselves inwardly that we are to lessen the number of insuperable temptations; by adapting ourselves to our environment rather than by attempting to adapt it to our weakness. And this is the task of that sane, rational asceticism which distinguishes the Gospel from the religions of Pessimism, with their false "mysticality" and their doctrine of radical antagonism between the spirit and the flesh. Where supernatural value is attached to morbid psychological conditions, it is easily supposed that a disregard and flagrant violation of all the laws of bodily health are conducive to the higher life of communion with God. That the hysterical phenomena deliberately induced by such "destruction of the body" are precisely paralleled by the effects of vice and of unbridled wilfulness of every kind, is evidence of a rationale common to both cases, namely, the splitting up and disintegration of the normal psychological harmony. The same result is obtained by any prolonged over-taxing of the mental faculties, whose weariness releases the lower nature from their control and suffers it to set up a rebel government of its own. In all such cases God, in nature, avenges the violation of the laws of reason, and leaves men prey to the countless illusions and degradations incident to the dismemberment of our moral personality.

Christian asceticism, on the other hand, unifies and co-ordinates body and soul with all their powers and faculties, and builds up that personality which consists in perfect self-determination; in the progressive mastery of spirit over nature both within us and outside us. But this is not accomplished without pain and daily mortification. The service of reason is the most costing of all. Habit makes the wildest austerities bearable and even unnoticeable; but the life of reason is ever demanding something new, something more, and opens fresh wounds far faster than habit can heal them. In a word, it is much easier to deaden and destroy the psychic nature than to train and perfect it; much easier to tyrannize over it than to govern it justly.

2

By no means are we taught to watch and pray against those temptations which are within our strength, which are the indispensable means of maintaining our strength: "Try me, O God," prays the Psalmist, "and seek the ground of my heart: prove me and examine my thoughts. See well if there be any way of wickedness in me, and lead me in the way everlasting" (Ps. CXXXVIII. 24). Under-exercise is as bad for our muscles as over-strain. A certain moderate strain is necessary for their development. The same holds good of our spiritual education. The mind that lies idle, or contents itself with the easy application of principles already possessed, that shrinks from grappling with new problems and from the labour of continual self-reformation, grows torpid and mechanical. The will that is not always struggling for some further degree of personality and self-mastery loses its vigour and begins to fall below its present measure of self-possession. Not to advance is to recede. Hence we always need some task a little more difficult than any we have hitherto accomplished; one that will educe the power already latent within us, and in so doing store up new power for some yet more difficult task. As money gets money, so every truth acquired by the mind brings new truths within our reach; and every conquest achieved by the will makes further conquests possible. This is an elementary principle of all rational education, as is plain from the graduated exercise books that we put into children's hands.

To protect ourselves from difficulties within our strength is to paralyse and cripple ourselves. It is spiritual cowardice and laziness, and nothing more. Far from avoiding, we must seek temptations of this sort for ourselves and for those whom we would educate mentally and morally as well as physically. Hence it is that our Lord says of His disciples: "I pray, not that Thou shouldest take them out of the world, but that Thou shouldest keep them from evil"; not that they should be delivered from difficulties, but from improportionate and insuperable difficulties. He who sent them forth as sheep into the midst of wolves, sent them into the very thick of temptation. And if He Himself fled the world for a season and went into the desert, it was not to fly temptation, but that He might be tempted of the devil, and come forth stronger than ever against the lesser temptations of the world.

X

THE SEVENTH PETITION

Sed libera nos a malo.—But deliver us from evil.

I

If our modes of theological expression are necessarily imperfect, owing to the improportion of our mind to the matter dealt with, they are doubly so when the deepest and most insoluble of all theological problems—the problem of evil—is in question. God must be the author of evil: God cannot possibly be the author of evil. Here are two irreconcilable conclusions that seem to force themselves with equal right on human reason. If we accept one of them, we must treat the other as an insoluble difficulty. We are not, then, and never can be, in so superior a position ourselves as to condemn out of hand a view of the matter which now seems to us misleading, and to have been wisely discarded in the later writings of the New Testament.

Combating a false but evidently common interpretation of the older presentments of this truth, St. James writes: " Let no man say when he is tempted, I am tempted of God, for God cannot be tempted of evil, and He Himself tempteth no man ; but each man is tempted when he is drawn away by his own lusts and enticed. Be not deceived, my beloved brethren ; every good gift and every perfect gift is from above, and cometh down from the Father of light, with whom can be no variation, neither shadow that is cast by turning" (James I. 13-17). God is the Father of the heavenly lights, of the stars, and of the angels whom they symbolize. He Himself knows no rising nor setting—nothing of that mutability which belongs to every finite will, but shines with a steady radiance, diffusing good, and only good, to all His creatures. As He Himself cannot vary or be tempted to evil, so neither can He tempt any man to evil, nor will that any shall die, but that all should come to repentance. Be not deceived; we may tempt ourselves, and others may tempt us, but God never tempts us.

On the other hand, it is equally true that nothing can evade God's providence; that it is He who permits, not only those strictly insuperable temptations which issue in material but blameless breaches of the moral law, but also those superable temptations which come to us from the world or the flesh; and even those sins which, in another sense, are due to the free opposition of our will to His.

This side of the truth was emphasized in the Old Testament mode of theological thought and expression. That God should tempt a man to sin, i.e. to transgress against Himself, is an intolerable thought for one who realizes the absolute unity and righteousness of God; but it is less intolerable in the measure that men conceive God humanwise in their own sinful image and likeness; and it was altogether tolerable for those heathen whose heaven was a pandemonium of intriguing deities, each jealous of the other's worshippers, and striving to sow discord. The sense of being victimized by a divine madness and forced into sin was familiar enough to those early Semitic neighbours whose religious language in many cases passed over to Israel with a new interpretation, yet always with a liability to return to the primitive sense on the lips of the carnal-minded and the pagan at heart.

That God tempted Abraham, that He hardened Pharaoh's heart, etc., were expressions easily, and no doubt frequently, misunderstood in a pagan sense. Hence we find temptation more and more explicitly ascribed to secondary causes, under the divine permission: to Satan and his angels. And as even this view of the matter encouraged men to excuse themselves and throw their blame on other shoulders—"the serpent beguiled me, and I did eat"—the tendency to seek the source of temptation in men's own hearts and imaginings becomes even in the Old Testament ever more pronounced, and in the New reaches its clearest expression in the passage just quoted from St. James.

The petition, "Lead us not into temptation," belongs to that older form of theological thought. It emphasizes the truth that our lots are in God's hands; that our very temptations are in His control; that no sparrow can fall to the ground without His will who feeds the sparrow; that as we stand, so we fall, only by His decree.

Still, the havoc that certain theories of predestination and predetermination have played with this divine truth justifies the needful explanation that the sixth petition of the Lord's Prayer receives in the seventh. St. Luke ends with "Lead us not into temptation"; St. Matthew adds the fuller explanation: "But deliver us from evil," or "from the evil one." God is not the tempter positively, but at most permissively; He does not lead us, but only suffers us to be led into temptation, in so much as He does not always deliver us from evil or from the Tempter.

2

The liturgical languages of the Church, East and West, leave it ambiguous whether we should read "from evil," or "from the evil one." Tertullian, Cyprian, and the Greek Fathers after Origen take the latter view; most of the Western authorities take the former, which has become popularized with us. Of the parallel passages in the New Testament where the same word occurs, seven demand the personal sense,[1] four are ambiguous,[2] and one only requires the impersonal sense.[3] When in addition to this we remember that the Lord's Prayer is the Prayer of the Kingdom of Heaven, whose establishment on earth entails the destruction of the Kingdom of Satan; when we read of the Tempter bargaining with Christ for the kingdoms of the world (Matt. IV. 8, 11); when we find the arch-principle of evil presented to us as a personality on every page of the Gospel and all through the New Testament; when, finally, we see in this seventh petition a probable assigning of temptation to its true origin—we have an overwhelming argument in favour of the rendering:

[1] Matt. XIII. 19, 38; 1 John II. 13, 14, III. 12, V. 18; Eph. VI. 18.
[2] Matt. V. 37; John XVII. 15; 2 Thess. III. 3; 1 John V. 19.
[3] Rom. XII. 9.

"But deliver us from the evil one," i.e. "Lead us not into temptation, but deliver us from the Tempter, from Satan."

So, no doubt, the first hearers will have understood the prayer. Yet between the understanding of it and the interpretation of it which has become current amongst ourselves there is no substantial or practical difference. As the Spirit and the fruits of the Spirit, so the devil and the works of the devil are the same thing for purposes of religious life and guidance. The metaphysical nature of the principles of evil and their mode of intervention are problems of speculative theology solved in different ways at different times. From those problems we simply prescind when we pray, "Deliver us from evil," rather than "from the evil one,"—"from the works of the devil," rather than "from the devil."

The "works of the devil," which Christ came to destroy in order that He might make us sons of God, of the Father in heaven, are the causes and results of the Kingdom of Satan. They stand for all that positive evil and disorder which the forces of uncurbed egoism have brought into the world; which are hostile to the interests of religion and morality; and which are the source and origin of those temptations against which we are taught to pray. This evil is within each of us, so far as vices and disorders of mind, imagination, feeling, affection, and passion limit our freedom and self-mastery, force us to do the things we would not, and hinder our doing what we would. It is also outside us in human society, so far as egoism has succeeded in organizing civilization and its institutions in its own interest to the prejudice of personal liberty and spiritual development, and has made the Kingdom of God and His righteousness subordinate to transitory ends. It is not in making the spiritual life difficult, but in making it insuperably difficult to so large a degree for such multitudes, that the world in its present state of disorder is styled the Kingdom of Satan. From such evil and suffering as has its root in sin and selfishness Christ has come to deliver us and to restore us to the liberty and self-command of the sons of God. And for this deliverance each Christian and the whole Christian Church must pray and work, ceaselessly and courageously, against the corruptive forces and the corrupt institutions of society—against the Kingdom or rule of Satan.

God's rule is that of a Father over sons who obey freely or actively because they choose, and because they love. Satan's rule is that of a tyrant over slaves who obey passively because they cannot help it, because their freedom is gone. In both cases, we have seen that the Kingdom is at once internal and external with respect to the spirit. When our trespasses are forgiven we are delivered from sin—from the inward rule of the devil. But so long as life lasts, and so long as the world lasts, man's spiritual liberty will always be fettered to some degree by disorders within and without; by the limitations of his own nature and by those of human society; by the flesh and by the world. However far we push the realm of our freedom and of God's external Kingdom on earth, there will always be a wall of darkness round our Goshen, a boundary beyond which our self-mastery may break down under stress of insuperable temptation. In view of such possibilities, not as already captives, but as free sons of God fighting for yet greater freedom, we pray: Deliver us from evil.

XI

RESULTS

I

We have treated the last clauses of the Lord's Prayer with greater brevity, lest the repeated and obvious application of the same governing ideas should grow wearisome. Enough has been said to give those ideas clear definition and to exhibit them concretely, as controlling action and life.

Our purpose was to enter into the spirit of that prayer as being the most authentic and deliberate self-utterance of the spirit of Christ; as giving us a key to the Gospels, and a revelation of the governing intuitions, affections, and aims of Christ's life upon earth; and as therefore defining for us that spirit-life whose development is a test of doctrinal truth just because doctrine is shaped by its exigencies and is but a statement of its intellectual implications.

In the course of our brief exposition we have seen enough to vindicate the character of true Christian devotion against the three perversions which we have stigmatized as Sentimentality, Mysticality, and Practicality; and to arrive at a positive conception of the whole truth in which these lying half-truths are redeemed.

We have seen that the spirit of Christ may be viewed as Feeling: that it is before all else a spirit of Love and Charity. But it is a feeling generated and determined by a clear vision of the deepest realities of the spiritual order; a feeling that is magnetically drawn to truth and repelled by error just because it wraps the eternal truth within itself; because it is the feeling of a heart that is absolutely pure and transparent. It is blind neither as to its Whence nor its Whither; it is a creation of Truth and a principle of Truth.

Nor is it inert, self-consuming, luxurious; but a feeling which blossoms in will, fructifies in action. It is a spiritual feeling, because its object is selfless and its aims are selfless. It is that love of divine and universal goodness, that longing for divine and universal ends, of which it is said: "The zeal of Thy House hath consumed me" and "Lord, I have loved the beauty of Thy House and the place where Thy glory dwelleth." It is a hunger and thirst after righteousness that rigorously subordinates every psychic self-regarding feeling and affection to its own satisfaction.

Yet what it subordinates it does not destroy, but perfects, elevates, strengthens. Under its firm discipline every best instinct of the psychic self attains to its richest development; because it is purged of its selfishness and pressed into the service of selfless love. To this the tender-hearted compassion of the Gospel Christ owes its spiritual depth and strength, which distinguish it from that soft, indiscriminate sympathy of effeminate natures, which weakens rather than braces the sufferer, which shrinks from the pain of inflicting wholesome pain, which refuses the control of foresight and reason, and is rather a lawless passion than a free act of the self-determining spirit.

It is precisely as illuminated by Reason and mastered by Will that Christ's Feeling is all divine, and is raised above the psychic to the spiritual plane. Selfishness is the corruption of Feeling as it is of the Mind and the Will. There is an "ought" of feeling, as of thinking and willing. For us to feel as we ought (i.e. to feel with God, to feel divinely) demands severe and continued discipline and self-resistance, by which the psychic man is slowly brought into harmony with the spiritual. To take our feelings as we find them, to obey our likes and dislikes blindly, is to go from bad to worse, and to forge fetters for our spiritual liberty. In Christ one free, over-mastering love held every other love captive in an iron grip. In reference to that ideal of right feeling, of feeling with God, we are, the best of us, *viatores*, travellers stumbling on our way: He was the *comprehensor*, safe at the journey's end. *Fiat pax in virtute tua:* in His strength He found peace; the peace of the sons of God.

Again, the spirit of Christ can be viewed as Vision, Intelligence, Understanding; as a Spirit of truth. If the pure of heart see God, perfection of purity implied perfection of vision. No man knoweth the Father but the Son, who is in the bosom of the Father, and who hath declared Him. The whole movement of our Saviour's life was governed and controlled by this ever-present vision; and we, too, are to walk in the Light, even as He is in the Light. In the Johannine writings He is presented to us principally under this aspect—as Light, Truth, Intelligence. As God is Light, so Christ is Light, and in Him is no darkness at all. And He is the Truth, even as God is the Truth.

As we must feel with God, so we must think with God. Every little fragment of truth, every little ray of light that enters our mind and mitigates its darkness, is a new degree of communion with God, a new appropriation of the Divine Life. A passion for truth, an antagonism to avoidable ignorance and error, is an inseparable characteristic of the spirit-life. For this was Christ born, for this came He into the world, for this He lived and for this He died—that He might bear witness to the truth. But truth must be loved purely, disinterestedly; not for psychic and selfish ends; not as useful or convenient in any narrow sense of utility. It must not be subjected to man as a means, but worshipped by him as an end, even as God. For if God is the Truth, so the Truth is He. In this the spiritual quest of right thinking is parallel to the spiritual quest of right feeling. The latter, too, has its psychic commodities and advantages—is useful in a lower conditional sense as well as in the higher absolute sense. But the spirit-life is a seeking of God for God's sake, a disinterested worship of the Ought in feeling, in thinking, in willing; a dying to self and a living to righteousness.

So to die demands a strength that God alone can give; a strength that makes us sons of God and more-than-men. It demands a courage which can say to Truth, "Lord, I will follow Thee whithersoever Thou goest"; which can leave positions of comfort and safety and step down fearlessly on the troubled waters when He says, "It is I; be not afraid." We have also seen that Christ's opposition to what was abstract, unreal, life-destroying in a theology that refused the check of religious experience and hardened itself against the quickening influences of the prophetic spirit, may not be construed into an opposition to theology in general, to the effort of the understanding to make explicit and systematize the implications of religious experience and co-ordinate them with the rest of human knowledge; that such understanding is an indispensable instrument of life, spiritual as well as temporal; that dogma in some form or other is the seed as well as the fruit of all religious experience. His own work on earth was to destroy the false theology of the scribes, rather than formulate the true, and to deliver to His Apostles a spirit of Truth whose implications could subsequently be unfolded into a theology as time and occasion might demand.

Yet of a false mysticism, straining curious eyes at the darkness that wraps the Godhead, spurning the psychic life and its limitations as wholly evil, falsifying the mind through the violation of its marriage with the body, confounding morbid with supernatural conditions of thought and feeling—of all this there is no sort of encouragement in the sane mysticism of the Gospel. The spirit-life is essentially supernatural and mystical; but it is also a strengthening and perfecting of the natural or psychic life. It recognizes the solidarity and continuity of heaven and earth; the permeation of the human by the divine; and, for all its relative and practical dualism, it believes in one God, Creator of heaven and earth, and of all things visible and invisible. Without in any sense subordinating right thinking to right feeling or willing, the spirit of Christ demands their co-ordination, and will not tolerate the preference of any one to the prejudice of the others. Each is dependent on the other two; all three together constitute the supernatural life. Hence the intellectualism of the false mystic which would cripple the will and dry up the fountains of feeling stands utterly condemned. The Light that was in Christ kindled straightway into Love, and broke forth into Will and Deed. Light is not given us for our solitary delectation; the Christian may not stand for ever gazing up into heaven, but must use the light he has received in the service of God's Kingdom. Moreover, of the two it is through work, through experience rather than through mental effort and much thinking, that the Christian is illuminated. Yet lessons of reflection and experience, as we have here said, must alternate if we are to escape illusion and unreality on the one side, shallowness and mere "practicality" on the other.

Finally, the spirit of Christ may be viewed in Will; as a spiritual force making for good; as a human will so freely identified with the divine as to be its pure unimpeded manifestation. For every act of right willing is an act of self-identification with

God, an appropriation of the Divine Life. In treating of Christian asceticism we have seen what a superhuman degree of strength such an annihilation of the psychic will involves; and we have learnt to look on Christ crucified and obedient unto death and to say, " This truly was the Son of God."

Viewed internally or externally, on its spiritual or on its earthly and visible side, we have seen that the Kingdom of Heaven suffers violence, and that only the violent can take it by storm. We have learnt the deeper and truer sense of the beatitude, " The meek shall possess the earth "—the self-conquered shall conquer. We have learnt to distinguish the true spiritual strength of God's sons, whose ultimate motive is self-chosen and self-imposed, from its psychic counterfeit, from the strength that derives from some one enslaving passion or instinct which presses all the others and even reason itself into its service, from the strength of fallen angels. It is by its own free act that the spirit appropriates and holds on to the Will of God, and brings all other ends and motives into subjection to the same.

But if such good will is beneficent in every direction as far as outer conditions favour its activity, yet we have learnt from Christ to value the internal spiritual act far more than its outward fruits; and to recognize that it is by the former alone that the spirit is characterized and constituted what it is; that works without faith are dead; and that this faith is inseparably bound up with right feeling and right thinking; in fine, that mere " practicality " is the religion of those who "have a name to live, but are dead."

2

But why so many words about a matter so simple and plain, except that it is just these simple elementary notions that are most elusive in every way, most easily sophisticated in the mind, most easily neglected in practice?

St. Paul has the whole matter in a few words when he says: "I live; now not I, but Christ liveth in me"—words whose sense is identical with those of the Gospel: "I in them, and Thou in Me." Here we have the clear distinction between two sorts of life with which the spirit can identify itself—the natural or psychic and the Divine or Christ life. In the latter its spiritual nature is realized; in the former it is destroyed. God lives in us just in the measure that by a free effort we rise above the self-interested individualistic standpoint and devote ourselves freely and disinterestedly to the service of goodness, truth, and love; just in the measure that we die to the psychic self and become simply and purely organs of the Divine Life. So that it is God or Christ who feels in us, who thinks in us, who wills in us.

That through ever proffered grace we are capable of such elevation is a matter of experience and observation. Especially when our private and separate interest is slightly affected or not at all, we are all of us, even the most degraded, capable at times of objective, disinterested judgments, feelings, resolutions, provided the cost be little. For others, unrelated to ourselves, we feel the imperative claims of conscience, the pressure of the " Ought " of feeling or thought or will; we can at least be roused to a sluggish zeal, a cheap indignation, in the cause of Truth and Right. Feebly and dimly we recognize that we are not mere splinters and fragments, but that the whole world lives in us, speaks in us—or that it ought to. But more than this, we constantly rise to a certain limit of self-sacrifice in the cause of God, and stand for odd moments and seasons high above the natural egoistic plane. Not till such moments are multiplied so thickly as to run into one another, like the vibrations that pass into a sustained note, not till the limits of self-sacrifice are wholly obliterated, does the spirit die into God and the psychic self become a mere memory as of a friend long since passed away, or of the home of our childhood to which we can return no more.

And if this utter absorption of the human will into the divine, this impossibility of return to the psychic level seems prejudicial to the essence of personality, let us remember that it is a self-imposed impossibility, effected and sustained by the spirit's own free act; that it is the triumph of a strength which grips God with an iron grasp; that it is the very highest achievement of personality and self-determination. For the same free act by which the spirit "differentiates" itself from nature identifies it with God. As against our fellows, separateness and opposition seem to be the very essence of personality, as they undoubtedly are of psychic self-hood. We rightly dread the passive subjection and slavery of one man's mind or will to that of another. We feel that the spirit so hypnotized is stupefied, debased, sterilized as by a vice; that the loss of distinctness is a forfeiture of dignity. And so far as we imagine God humanwise, as a psychic unit, the utter subjection of the spirit to Him suggests a like forfeiture. But we must remember that besides the possible spiritual dependence of the inert and feeble-minded on stronger individuals, there is a free, self-determined adhesion to the mind and will of another, as to a higher manifestation of divine truth and goodness than we ourselves have yet attained. In such union we feel that personality is not lost but gained; that the spirit is not less itself but more; for its subjection is not to the individual, but to the universal and divine in the individual. And so of that absolute and direct subjection of the soul to God, which is the far-off ideal of spirit-life. Freedom and victory over nature mean self-enslavement to God; distinctness from the lower means identification with the higher. Such self-enslavement is the act by which the sons of God win and maintain their identity and personality. The spirit must choose between slavery and slavery—whether it is to be passively enslaved to nature, or to enslave itself freely to God.

Such, then, is that Love or Charity which is the New Testament expression for the spirit of Christ. If we have avoided those terms it is only because Love is so easily misunderstood in a sentimental or else a pseudo-mystical sense; and because Charity has grown cold and become a synonym for practicality and the business of philanthropy. Yet Love it is, in the wisest, tenderest, and strongest sense; that love by which God in us embraces Himself and all that proceeds from Himself. Simple as it is, its simplicity is that of divine fulness, not that of barren monotony. The variety of its applications, the depth of its implications are inexhaustible. All that has been shown us of its manifestations in the life of Christ and of His mystical body, the Church of the Just in every age and clime, leaves infinitely more to be learnt. Yet even in the least word or deed of Christ, His spirit stands revealed for those who have eyes to see, so that the whole series of the Gospel narratives offers us abundant means of studying it, as we have been doing, from a hundred different aspects and of reaching the same end from a hundred different approaches. In its form, its modes of thought and language, the Gospel necessarily belongs to a certain time and place; but in its substance it belongs to eternity. It gives us the very essence of religion: human and divine, external and internal. the one thing needful.

CONCLUSION

LEX ORANDI

"VIEWED from the standpoint taken in these pages, tested by the criterions of life, of spiritual fruitfulness, the truths of Christianity cannot be expected to present the same precision and clearness of outline as when deduced from defined premises, and built up into a coherent intellectual system. We can but see men as trees walking; blurred contours; mountain shapes looming through mist. Yet the verification is not valueless; it is not nothing, if approaching the truth from this side, and by this less frequented path we find what we had a right to expect; it is not nothing if that vague 'Power which makes for righteousness' in the souls of men is seen, as we strain through darkness, to shape itself ever more and more into conformity with the familiar beliefs of the Christian tradition."[1] I think it well to insist upon this point again, lest an emphasis of the apologetic importance of religious experience should be misconstrued into an underrating of the importance of reflection and reasoning; lest steering clear of Intellectualism we should be engulfed in "Voluntarism" or some untenable form of Pragmatism.

[1] "Lex Orandi," p. xxxi.

That the truth of a dogma is simply and only practical; that it means merely "act *as if* this were true, and you will act aright"; that it is nothing more than an ethical myth—is a position which I have repeatedly repudiated in "Lex Orandi" wherever I have insisted that a belief which constantly and universally fosters spiritual life must so far be true to the realities of the spiritual world, and must therefore possess a representative as well as a practical value. If there is a Pragmatism that denies this, I have nothing to do with it. Still I have equally insisted that such representations are almost necessarily analogies or even symbols. And since there may be two analogies of the same truth, whose literal values are contradictory, it follows that the "Law of Prayer" might easily give us very different creeds of just the same religious value—all equally true to the practical needs of the spirit-life, and analogously representative of the spiritual world. If the Creed is principally the product of the Church's spiritual life, yet other causes have collaborated. Indeed, as we have said, the spirit of prayer is selective rather than creative, and works on materials ready to hand, modifying and correcting existing beliefs according to its own exigencies. And what it thus selects and gathers together lacks the unity of a theological system. Its unity is that of varied utterances and manifestations of the same spirit; such, for example, as pervades the inspired writings of the prophets. Its language is literary rather than scientific; its utterances taken at their literal value are often irreconcilable, just because their truth is that of analogy.

But here it is that theological reflection comes in and begins its delicate task of striving to get at the intellectual implications of the spirit of prayer as revealed in all this prophetic utterance ; to create a thought-system which by explaining will enable us to control and extend our spiritual experience, and which will serve religion in the same way that science serves life. That it often fails, that if often sterilizes rather than fertilizes, is the fault, not of theology, but of the theologian.

Our Creed, therefore, is the joint work of Theology and Devotion ; of reflection and life. We cannot prove, then, that in form and substance it has been shaped solely by the exigencies of prayer in all its details ; nor that those exigencies could not have been satisfied by some other equivalent representation of the spiritual world. All we contend is that a Creed has representative truth so far as it constantly and universally fosters the spirit-life ; that it is false so far as it is spiritually sterilizing and decadent. That takes us but a little way towards the apologist's end. There are other kinds of truth which the Creed claims to possess, and of which the " Lex Orandi " can offer no criterion. Of these, theology proper must undertake the defence. Thus, the " Prayer-value " of certain historical beliefs cannot demonstrably be shown to depend on the historicity of the facts, which therefore must be determined otherwise, namely, by the ordinary apologetic methods. It is not however so much in the interests of Theology as in those of Devotion that I have tried to make clear the relation between the Church's spiritual life and her theological reflection, and to show their dependence on one another. What we may call the theological temper and the devotional temper are very different, and each is only too ready to go its own way with a certain impatience and even disdain of the other. So far, then, as a propensity to Intellectualism on the part of the theologian tends to alienate the practical and devout Christian from Theology altogether, it is timely to insist on the general subordination of Theology to Devotion, and to show that the Creed is ultimately a creation and an instrument of the Church's spiritual life; that if reason too has had a hand in its production, yet it has been only as the servant of Devotion, which is the principal agent.

If, then, that Intellectualism errs which follows its own dialectic without respect to experience, and endeavours to drag the Spirit along paths determined *a priori* by hard reasoning, that Pragmatism errs no less which ignores the relation of mutual dependence between experience and reflection; which fails to see that understanding increases our possibilities of experience, just as experience increases our possibilities of understanding; that dogma, of some sort or other, is both parent and child of action, just as action is both parent and child of dogma. We shall perhaps grasp the relation less awkwardly if we regard reflection and experience as parallel processes of the spirit-life rather than as alternating moments of the same process. Experience borrows its "form" from reflection; reflection its "matter" from experience. But each process—the thought which is lived and the life which is thought—pursues its own course and is governed by its own laws, dependent on the other, yet apart from the other. They are as helpful neighbours, rendering one another indispensable services, and to whom a quarrel is equally detrimental.

The difficulty of a correct view arises from our necessity of thinking and speaking as though Vision, Feeling, and Will were separable and successive acts of the spirit-life, and not simply aspects of one and the same act; as though one were afore or after the other, whereas all are simultaneous and co-equal, because they are all one. Not without reason have the Fathers sought in various ways for an image of the Trinity in the spirit of man.

Plainly, then, it would be a complete misapprehension of the scope of "Lex Orandi" were one to sit down and sift every point of Catholic belief, with a view to rejecting those that did not manifestly stand the "Pragmatic" test, or even were one to endeavour to deduce a creed *a priori* from the known exigencies of the spirit-life. Its purpose was not to supply a new theological weapon, or a criterion for violent and artificial criticism, but to furnish a reason for trusting to the natural criticism effected by Time and Experience; for suffering Good and Evil to grow together till the harvest; for quietly abiding the sure uprooting of every plant not planted by the Father's hand; for living the Truth rather than analysing it.

The rough and seemingly cruel methods of Nature, the struggle for existence, the elimination of the weak and worthless, may not be too summarily excluded from the moral and spiritual domain. Reformers, whether of doctrine or discipline, are often the worst enemies of reform through palliatives that protract rather than cure the evils they would remedy. Often the shortest, the kindest, the most effectual remedy for abuses is not to weed them out, but to let them grow and manifest their true natures, and work their own destruction. Without warranting fatalistic apathy or inertness, or cooling the reformer's zeal, faith in the wise methods of Nature, faith in God, who works in and through those methods, would impart a very different direction to his efforts in many cases.

.   .   .   .   .

Thus, then, we reach our goal, which was to determine more exactly what we meant by the "spirit of Christ" when we maintained that religious beliefs which constantly and universally fostered that spirit in us were thereby proved to be true to the laws of our eternal and supernatural life, and to be at least analogously representative of the realities of the world to which that life relates us.

Such are the beliefs of the Gospel upon which our whole creed is built up,—the doctrine of the Kingdom of Heaven, of the Eternal Father, the only begotten Son, the Holy Spirit of adoption, the Communion of Saints, the Forgiveness of sins, the Resurrection of the body, and Life everlasting.